YOUTUBE MASTERY

The Ultimate Guide to Building a Successful & Profitable Channel

Gabriel Williams

Table of Contents

INTRODUCTION

YouTube has become a powerhouse in the digital age, providing a platform for creative individuals like you to share your passions, talents, and expertise with the world. With billions of active users and countless hours of video content consumed every day, YouTube offers an unprecedented opportunity to connect with a global audience and turn your dreams into reality.

But here's the thing: starting a YouTube channel and achieving success is not just about posting a few videos and hoping for the best. It takes careful planning, strategic execution, and a deep understanding of the platform and its nuances. That's where this book comes in.

In this comprehensive guide, we'll walk through everything you need to know to kick-start your YouTube journey. Whether you want to become a vlogging sensation, a gaming guru, a beauty expert, or anything else you can imagine, this book will provide you with the tools, strategies, and insights to help you achieve your goals.

We'll start by understanding the power and potential of YouTube, exploring why it has become the go-to platform for content creators worldwide. From there, we'll delve into finding your niche and identifying your target audience, because knowing who you're creating content for is essential for success.

Once we have the foundation set, I'll guide you through the process of setting up your YouTube channel and optimizing it to attract viewers and subscribers. You'll learn the art of content creation, including planning, filming, editing, and optimizing your videos to stand out from the crowd.

But YouTube is not just a one-way street. It's about building a community, engaging with your audience, and fostering meaningful connections. We'll explore strategies for building an engaged community, promoting your channel, and monetizing your content to turn your passion into a profitable venture.

Of course, success on YouTube doesn't happen overnight. We'll uncover the secrets of growing your channel, increasing subscribers, and managing your channel for long-term success. We'll also discuss the ever-evolving landscape of YouTube, including emerging trends and staying ahead of the game.

Chapter 1

UNDERSTANDING YOUTUBE: A POWERFUL PLATFORM FOR CONTENT CREATORS

YouTube has revolutionized the way we consume and interact with media. It has provided a democratic space where anyone with a camera and an internet connection can showcase their talents, express their opinions, and connect with a global audience. As a content creator, understanding the power and influence of YouTube is paramount to your success. In this chapter, we shall look into the rise and popularity of YouTube. Then we shall discuss why it is good to start a YouTube channel, seeing YouTube as a business opportunity and the types of YouTube channels you may want to consider; equipping you with the background knowledge you need to get started. Let's dive right into it.

THE RISE AND POPULARITY OF YOUTUBE

To truly understand the immense power and potential of YouTube, we must first take a step back and explore its extraordinary rise to prominence in the digital landscape.

YouTube emerged onto the scene in February 2005, founded by three former PayPal employees who recognized the need for a platform that allowed users to easily share and watch videos online. Little did they know that their creation would revolutionize the way we consume and create content forever.

In its early days, YouTube was a playground for viral videos, funny clips, and amateur content. It quickly gained traction and captured the attention of millions, who flocked to the platform in search of entertainment and a place to share their own videos with the world.

Over the years, YouTube underwent a remarkable transformation. It evolved from a casual video-sharing website into a global phenomenon that influences culture, shapes trends, and provides an income stream for countless creators. Today, it stands as the second-largest search engine in the world, trailing only its parent company, Google.

What fueled YouTube's explosive growth and enduring popularity? The answer lies in its unique combination of accessibility, interactivity, and limitless possibilities. YouTube transcends borders, cultures, and languages, connecting people from all corners of the globe through the power of video.

The platform's user-friendly interface and intuitive features make it easy for anyone to upload and watch videos. Whether you're a tech-savvy teenager or a retiree exploring a new hobby, YouTube welcomes creators of all backgrounds and skill levels.

What truly sets YouTube apart is its unrivaled sense of community. It's not just a passive viewing experience; it's a vibrant ecosystem where viewers can engage with creators, share their thoughts, and even contribute to the content itself. The comment section beneath every video serves as a virtual meeting place, fostering conversations, and building relationships.

The impact of YouTube reaches far beyond mere entertainment. It has become a powerful educational tool, allowing people to learn new skills, acquire knowledge, and expand their horizons. From DIY tutorials to language lessons, from cooking tips to fitness routines, YouTube has become a go-to resource for learning and personal growth.

Moreover, YouTube has spawned a new generation of celebrities and influencers. Individuals who started with humble beginnings, armed with nothing more than a camera and a dream, have risen to fame, amassed millions of subscribers, and built lucrative careers. YouTube has democratized fame, giving everyone a shot at success, regardless of their background or connections.

The rise of YouTube has also been propelled by technological advancements. The proliferation of smartphones, high-speed internet, and affordable video equipment has made it easier than ever to create and consume content. The barrier to entry has been significantly lowered, allowing aspiring creators to enter the YouTube arena with minimal investment.

In essence, YouTube is a platform that thrives on creativity, authenticity, and the power of storytelling. It has transformed ordinary individuals into influential voices, challenging traditional media channels and democratizing content creation.

As we embark on this journey to master YouTube, it's crucial to recognize the remarkable rise and popularity of this platform. It is a testament to the boundless opportunities that await us as we take our first steps towards building a successful and profitable YouTube channel. So, let's dive in and unlock the secrets to YouTube success together.

WHY START A YOUTUBE CHANNEL?

So, you might be wondering why you should start a YouTube channel in the first place. What sets it apart from other forms of content creation and why should you invest your time, energy, and creativity into building a presence on this platform? Well, let me give you a few compelling reasons.

1. Reach a Global Audience: YouTube has a staggering number of active users, with billions of people visiting the platform every month. Whether you want to share your passion for fashion, gaming, cooking, or any other niche, YouTube provides you with an opportunity to connect with a massive global audience. The potential for reaching people from different cultures, backgrounds, and corners of the world is unparalleled.

2. Showcase Your Creativity and Expertise: YouTube is a blank canvas waiting for you to unleash your creative ideas and talents. It allows you to express yourself, share your knowledge, and demonstrate your skills in a visually captivating way. Whether you're a musician, a filmmaker, a comedian, or an educator, YouTube gives you a platform to showcase your unique abilities and leave a lasting impact on viewers.

3. Build a Personal Brand: In today's digital age, personal branding has become increasingly important. By starting a YouTube channel, you have the opportunity to shape your own personal brand and establish yourself as an authority in your chosen field. Consistently creating valuable and engaging content helps you build credibility, gain recognition, and open doors to exciting opportunities, both online and offline.

4. Monetization and Income Potential: Let's not ignore the financial aspect of starting a YouTube channel. While it may take time and effort to build a substantial income, YouTube offers various monetization options that can turn your channel into a profitable venture. Through advertising revenue, sponsorships, merchandise sales, and other income streams, successful YouTubers have been able to generate significant income and even make it their full-time career.

5. Engage with a Community: One of the most fulfilling aspects of being a YouTuber is the ability to create a loyal and engaged community. YouTube provides a platform for meaningful interactions, allowing you to connect with your audience, receive feedback, answer questions, and even collaborate with other creators. Building relationships with your viewers can be immensely rewarding and can lead to lifelong friendships and support networks.

6. Learn and Grow: Starting a YouTube channel is a journey of continuous learning and personal growth. You'll develop new skills in content

creation, video editing, storytelling, and audience engagement. Along the way, you'll gain valuable insights into digital marketing, analytics, and trends that can be applied to various aspects of your life and career.

7. Leave a Lasting Legacy: YouTube allows you to create a lasting impact on the world. Your videos can inspire, educate, entertain, and empower people long after they are published. You have the opportunity to make a difference in someone's life, whether it's by sharing a heartfelt story, providing valuable advice, or simply bringing joy to their day. The ability to leave a positive mark on the world is truly remarkable.

These are just a few reasons why starting a YouTube channel is an incredible opportunity worth pursuing. It offers a unique blend of creative expression, personal growth, community engagement, and even financial rewards.

YOUTUBE AS A BUSINESS OPPORTUNITY

In addition to being a platform for creative expression and community engagement, YouTube offers a tremendous business opportunity for those willing to put in the effort and dedication. It has become a legitimate avenue for individuals to turn their passion into a profitable enterprise. Here's why YouTube can be a game-changer for aspiring entrepreneurs:

1. Diverse Monetization Options: YouTube provides various ways to monetize your content and

generate income. The most well-known method is through the YouTube Partner Program, which allows you to earn money from advertisements displayed on your videos. As your channel grows, you can also explore additional revenue streams such as sponsored content, brand partnerships, merchandise sales, crowdfunding, and even hosting live events or workshops. The ability to diversify your income sources gives you greater financial stability and flexibility.

2. Global Reach and Exposure: YouTube's global audience and immense reach offer unparalleled exposure for your brand and products. By creating valuable and engaging content, you can attract viewers from around the world, expanding your customer base beyond geographical boundaries. With the right marketing strategies, you can leverage YouTube's vast user base to grow your brand, increase visibility, and reach potential customers who might not have discovered you through traditional marketing channels.

3. Targeted Advertising Opportunities: YouTube's robust advertising platform allows businesses to run highly targeted ads to reach their ideal customers. By leveraging demographic data, interests, and search history, you can ensure that your ads are shown to the right audience, maximizing the chances of conversion and ROI. Whether you're promoting your own products or working with advertisers, YouTube's advertising

capabilities provide a powerful tool for reaching your target market.

4. SEO Benefits and Increased Online Presence: YouTube videos often rank high in search engine results, giving you an opportunity to boost your online presence and drive traffic to your website or other online platforms. By optimizing your video titles, descriptions, and tags with relevant keywords, you increase the visibility of your content in search results, attracting potential customers who are actively searching for related information. The increased exposure not only benefits your YouTube channel but also strengthens your overall online presence.

5. Market Research and Consumer Insights: YouTube offers a wealth of market research and consumer insights that can help you better understand your target audience. Through analytics, you can gather valuable data on viewer demographics, interests, engagement metrics, and even viewer feedback through comments. These insights provide valuable feedback on your content, allowing you to refine your strategies, tailor your offerings, and make data-driven decisions to better serve your audience.

6. Building a Recognizable Brand: YouTube provides an ideal platform to establish and build your brand identity. By consistently creating high-quality content that aligns with your brand values, you can differentiate yourself from competitors and cultivate a loyal following. As your brand gains recognition and trust, it becomes a valuable

asset that can open doors to partnerships, collaborations, and sponsorship opportunities with other businesses in your industry.

7. Personal and Professional Growth: Building a YouTube channel as a business venture offers tremendous personal and professional growth opportunities. You'll develop skills in content creation, video production, digital marketing, audience engagement, and business management. The challenges and successes you encounter along the way will shape you as an entrepreneur, teaching you resilience, adaptability, and valuable lessons that can be applied to future endeavors.

It's important to note that building a successful YouTube business requires dedication, consistency, and a well-thought-out strategy. It's not an overnight success story, but with perseverance and the right approach, YouTube can become a viable and rewarding business venture.

So, whether you're a solopreneur, a small business owner, or an aspiring influencer, YouTube offers an incredible business opportunity. It's time to leverage the power of this platform, embrace your entrepreneurial spirit, and embark on a journey towards building a thriving YouTube business. The possibilities are limitless, and the rewards can be truly life-changing.

TYPES OF YOUTUBE CHANNELS

When it comes to starting a YouTube channel, there is a wide range of content categories to choose from.

Finding the right niche that aligns with your passions, expertise, and target audience is essential for building a successful and engaging channel. Here are some popular types of YouTube channels to consider:

1. Vlogs and Lifestyle Channels: Vlogs (video blogs) have gained immense popularity on YouTube. These channels focus on documenting the daily lives, experiences, and adventures of the content creator. From travel vlogs to day-in-the-life vlogs, this format allows viewers to get a glimpse into the creator's world and form a personal connection.

2. Gaming Channels: Gaming channels have exploded in popularity, attracting millions of subscribers who are passionate about video games. Whether you're a gamer showcasing your skills, providing game reviews and tutorials, or entertaining viewers with humorous commentary, gaming channels provide a vast community of like-minded individuals.

3. Beauty and Fashion Channels: Beauty and fashion channels cater to those passionate about makeup, skincare, haircare, and style. These channels offer product reviews, tutorials, hauls, and tips for achieving different looks. From makeup enthusiasts to professional stylists, the beauty and fashion niche provides endless opportunities for creativity and collaboration.

4. Educational and How-To Channels: Educational channels cater to viewers seeking knowledge and learning opportunities. From science experiments

to language lessons, from historical documentaries to DIY projects, educational channels provide valuable and informative content in an engaging and accessible format.

5. Comedy and Entertainment Channels: Laughter is a universal language, and comedy and entertainment channels aim to entertain and bring joy to viewers. From sketch comedy to comedic commentary on trending topics, these channels rely on humor and creativity to engage and captivate audiences.

6. Fitness and Health Channels: With a growing emphasis on wellness, fitness, and healthy living, fitness and health channels have gained substantial popularity. These channels offer workout routines, nutrition tips, motivational content, and guidance on leading a healthy lifestyle. Whether you're a certified fitness trainer or a fitness enthusiast sharing your personal journey, this niche offers an opportunity to inspire and help others achieve their fitness goals.

7. Food and Cooking Channels: Food and cooking channels provide a feast for the eyes and the taste buds. These channels feature recipes, cooking tutorials, culinary adventures, and food-related content. From gourmet meals to quick and easy recipes, food channels cater to a wide range of viewers with diverse culinary interests.

8. Travel and Adventure Channels: Travel and adventure channels take viewers on a virtual journey to breathtaking destinations. These

channels showcase travel experiences, provide travel tips, and inspire viewers to explore the world. Whether you're a globetrotter capturing your adventures or a travel expert sharing insights, this niche allows you to share the wonders of the world with your audience.

These are just a few examples of the types of YouTube channels you can create. Remember, finding your niche is crucial for building a loyal and engaged audience. Consider your passions, expertise, and target audience to determine the content category that resonates with you the most. With dedication and a genuine love for your chosen niche, you'll be well on your way to creating a successful YouTube channel.

Chapter 2

FINDING YOUR NICHE AND IDENTIFYING YOUR TARGET AUDIENCE

As you embark on your YouTube journey, it's essential to explore various niches to find the one that aligns with your interests, expertise, and audience. Let's look into some popular YouTube niches that offer unique opportunities for content creation:

1. Tech and Gadgets: The tech niche is ever-evolving and caters to tech enthusiasts, gadget lovers, and those seeking the latest innovations. You can review smartphones, laptops, gaming consoles, and other tech products, provide tutorials on software and apps, or delve into emerging technologies like artificial intelligence or virtual reality.

2. Personal Development and Motivation: Personal development channels focus on empowering individuals to improve their lives, achieve goals, and develop a positive mindset. You can provide motivational speeches, share strategies for personal growth, offer productivity tips, and guide viewers in overcoming challenges.

3. Parenting and Family: Parenting channels provide valuable insights, tips, and experiences for parents, soon-to-be parents, or caregivers. You can discuss topics like pregnancy, newborn

care, child development, parenting hacks, and family activities. Sharing personal stories and offering practical advice can resonate with viewers navigating the joys and challenges of raising a family.

4. DIY and Crafts: DIY and crafts channels inspire creativity and provide step-by-step tutorials for various projects. Whether it's home decor, crafting, sewing, woodworking, or upcycling, this niche appeals to individuals looking for hands-on activities and creative inspiration.

5. Finance and Investing: Finance channels cater to individuals seeking financial advice, money management tips, and investment strategies. You can educate viewers about budgeting, saving, investing, and planning for retirement. Sharing insights on personal finance, cryptocurrency, or stock market trends can help viewers make informed financial decisions.

6. Music and Musical Instruments: If you have a passion for music, consider starting a channel focused on music tutorials, instrument reviews, song covers, or original compositions. You can provide guidance on playing specific instruments, share music theory lessons, or explore different music genres and their history.

7. Book Reviews and Literature: Book review channels offer literary enthusiasts a platform to discuss their favorite books, share recommendations, and provide in-depth analysis. You can explore various genres, interview

authors, and participate in book-related discussions, fostering a community of book lovers.

8. Language Learning: Language learning channels cater to individuals interested in acquiring new language skills. You can create video lessons, language pronunciation guides, cultural insights, and tips for effective language learning techniques. This niche allows you to connect with a diverse global audience.

9. Sports and Fitness: Sports and fitness channels focus on workouts, training techniques, sports analysis, and athlete profiles. Whether you're a professional athlete, a fitness coach, or a sports enthusiast, you can share your expertise, inspire viewers to lead an active lifestyle, and offer guidance on reaching fitness goals.

10. Travel Hacks and Tips: Travel-related channels provide valuable insights, travel hacks, destination guides, and tips for planning memorable trips. You can share your travel experiences, provide budget travel advice, showcase hidden gems, and offer practical information to help viewers make the most of their travel adventures.

Remember, these are just a few examples, and there are countless other niches waiting to be explored. The key is to choose a niche that resonates with your passion, knowledge, and ability to deliver engaging content. Conduct thorough research, evaluate your own interests and expertise, and consider the needs and preferences of your target audience. By finding the right niche, you'll be well on your way to building a successful YouTube channel that captivates and inspires viewers.

RESEARCHING AND ANALYZING YOUR TARGET AUDIENCE

Understanding your target audience is crucial for creating content that resonates with them and building a loyal and engaged YouTube community. Here are some steps to help you research and analyze your target audience effectively:

1. Define Your Ideal Viewer: Start by envisioning who your ideal viewer is. Consider their age, gender, interests, occupation, and demographics. Think about what challenges, needs, or interests they might have that your content can address. Developing a clear picture of your target audience will guide your content creation and marketing strategies.

2. Conduct Market Research: Use online tools, surveys, and social media analytics to gather data on your target audience. Look for information on their preferences, behaviors, and content consumption habits. Identify popular YouTube channels or influencers that attract a similar audience and study their content and engagement patterns.

3. Analyze YouTube Analytics: YouTube provides valuable analytics data that can offer insights into your audience's behavior. Explore metrics such as viewer demographics, watch time, traffic sources, and audience retention. Pay attention to

the performance of specific videos to understand which topics or formats resonate the most with your viewers.

4. Engage with Your Viewers: Actively engage with your viewers through comments, messages, and social media platforms. Encourage feedback, ask for suggestions, and listen to their opinions. This direct interaction allows you to gain deeper insights into their preferences, interests, and challenges, helping you refine your content and build stronger connections.

5. Use Keyword Research Tools: Utilize keyword research tools to identify popular search terms and topics within your niche. This data can guide your content creation and help you optimize your video titles, descriptions, and tags to improve discoverability and attract the right audience.

6. Monitor Social Media: Keep an eye on social media platforms to stay updated on trends, conversations, and discussions relevant to your target audience. Pay attention to hashtags, online communities, and influencers within your niche. Engaging in these conversations can provide valuable insights and help you tailor your content to meet your audience's needs.

7. Analyze Competitors: Study successful YouTube channels within your niche and analyze their content, engagement, and audience. Identify what sets them apart and how they cater to their viewers. Take note of the topics, formats, and

storytelling techniques that resonate with their audience and adapt them to fit your unique style.

8. Create Viewer Personas: Develop detailed viewer personas based on your research and analysis. These personas represent fictional representations of your target audience segments and include their demographics, interests, motivations, and pain points. Use these personas as references when creating content to ensure you're addressing the specific needs and preferences of each segment.

By conducting thorough research and analysis of your target audience, you can gain valuable insights that will shape your content strategy, improve engagement, and attract the right viewers. Remember that audience preferences may evolve over time, so it's important to continually monitor and adapt your content to meet their changing needs. Building a deep understanding of your target audience will help you create content that resonates, fosters community, and establishes your YouTube channel as a go-to resource within your niche.

DEFINING YOUR UNIQUE SELLING PROPOSITION (USP)

In a crowded YouTube landscape, it's crucial to have a Unique Selling Proposition (USP) that sets your channel apart and attracts viewers. Your USP is what makes your content unique, valuable, and differentiates you from competitors. Here are some steps to help you define your USP:

1. Identify Your Strengths: Start by identifying your strengths, skills, and unique qualities that you can bring to your YouTube channel. Consider your expertise, experiences, and passions. What sets you apart from others in your niche? This could be your knowledge in a specific subject, your creative storytelling abilities, or your charismatic on-camera presence.

2. Understand Your Audience's Needs: Gain a deep understanding of your target audience's needs, desires, and pain points. What challenges or problems do they face? How can your content address these needs and provide solutions? By aligning your USP with your audience's needs, you can offer valuable content that resonates with them.

3. Research Your Competitors: Study successful YouTube channels within your niche and analyze their content and USPs. Look for gaps or opportunities that they might have overlooked. This will help you carve out a unique position in the market by offering something different or approaching the topic from a fresh perspective.

4. Define Your Core Message: Develop a clear and compelling core message that encapsulates what your channel is about and the value it provides. This message should resonate with your target audience and communicate the unique benefits they can expect from your content. It should answer the question: "Why should viewers choose your channel over others?"

5. Emphasize Your Unique Approach: Determine how you can present your content in a unique and compelling way. This could involve using innovative storytelling techniques, incorporating humor or personal anecdotes, or presenting complex information in a simplified manner. Find ways to differentiate your content delivery style and make it memorable for your viewers.

6. Leverage Your Personality: Your personality is a powerful asset that can set you apart from other creators. Embrace your authentic self and let your personality shine through in your videos. Be relatable, genuine, and build a connection with your audience. Your personality can become an integral part of your USP, creating a loyal following that resonates with you on a personal level.

7. Consistency and Quality: Consistency and quality are key components of your USP. Strive to deliver content consistently, whether it's through regular upload schedules or maintaining a consistent tone and style. Additionally, ensure that your content is of high quality, with professional production values and attention to detail. This commitment to consistency and quality will help build trust and credibility with your audience.

8. Test and Iterate: As you define your USP, it's important to test and iterate based on audience feedback and analytics data. Pay attention to viewer engagement, comments, and video performance to understand what resonates with your audience. Be open to evolving your USP

over time to meet changing audience preferences and market dynamics.

Remember, your USP should be genuine and aligned with your passions and expertise. It's about showcasing your unique value and creating a memorable experience for your viewers. By defining and consistently delivering on your USP, you'll attract a loyal and engaged audience that recognizes and appreciates the distinctive qualities of your YouTube channel.

Chapter 3

SETTING UP YOUR YOUTUBE CHANNEL

To kick start your dream YouTube channel you will need to set up your account. Setting up your YouTube channel is the foundation of your online presence as a content creator. It is the digital home where your videos reside and where viewers come to discover your content. Follow me in this chapter as we dive into every step to take in order to set up your YouTube channel for a long-term success.

CREATING A GOOGLE ACCOUNT

Creating a Google Account is the first step towards starting your YouTube journey. A Google Account not only allows you to access various Google services, but it also provides you with the necessary credentials to create and manage your YouTube channel. Here's a step-by-step guide to help you create a Google Account:

1. Go to the Google Account creation page: Open your web browser and navigate to the Google Account creation page at https://accounts.google.com/signup.

2. Fill in your personal information: On the account creation page, you'll see a form asking for your personal information. Enter your first and last name in the respective fields.

3. Choose a username: Your username will be the email address associated with your Google

Account. You can either create a new email address specifically for your YouTube channel or use an existing one. If you choose to create a new email address, click on the "Create a new email address" link, and follow the prompts to set up a new Gmail address. If you prefer to use an existing email address, enter it in the "Username" field.

4. Create a strong password: Choose a strong and secure password for your Google Account. Make sure it's a combination of letters, numbers, and special characters to enhance security.

5. Complete your phone number and recovery email: Providing a phone number and recovery email address is optional but recommended. These can be used for account recovery purposes or additional security measures.

6. Verify your account: Google may require you to verify your account through a phone number or email. Follow the prompts to complete the verification process.

7. Accept the terms and conditions: Read and accept Google's terms of service and privacy policy. It's essential to familiarize yourself with these policies to ensure compliance and understand how your information will be used.

8. Set up your account preferences: After creating your Google Account, you can customize your account preferences, such as language, privacy settings, and personalization options. Take some

time to review these settings and adjust them according to your preferences.

Congratulations! You've successfully created a Google Account. Now, you can use this account to access various Google services, including YouTube. To create your YouTube channel, simply sign in to your Google Account and visit https://www.youtube.com/create_channel. Follow the on-screen prompts to set up and customize your YouTube channel.

Remember to keep your Google Account login credentials secure and regularly update your password to protect your account from unauthorized access. With your Google Account and YouTube channel ready, you're one step closer to sharing your unique content with the world!

SETTING UP YOUR YOUTUBE CHANNEL

Setting up your YouTube channel is an exciting step towards sharing your content with the world. Follow these steps to create and customize your YouTube channel:

1. Sign in to your Google Account: Visit https://www.youtube.com and sign in using the Google Account you created in the previous section.

2. Access YouTube Studio: Once signed in, click on your profile picture or avatar icon in the top-right corner of the screen. In the dropdown menu, select "YouTube Studio."

3. Create your channel: In YouTube Studio, click on the "Create" button located in the top-right corner of the screen. Select "Channel" from the dropdown menu.

4. Choose a channel name: On the "Create a channel" screen, you'll be prompted to choose a channel name. This name represents your YouTube brand and should reflect the content you plan to create. You can use your personal name, a business name, or a creative name that aligns with your niche.

5. Customize your channel: After creating your channel, it's time to customize its appearance and settings. Click on the "Customize Channel" button to access the customization options.

a. Channel art: Add a visually appealing banner or channel art that represents your brand. The recommended size for channel art is 2560 x 1440 pixels. Ensure that your artwork reflects your channel's theme and visually communicates your content.

b. Profile picture: Upload a profile picture that represents you or your brand. This image will appear next to your channel name in search results and comments. The recommended size for a profile picture is 800 x 800 pixels.

c. Channel trailer: Consider creating a channel trailer— a short video that introduces new viewers to your channel and gives them a taste of what they can expect. Showcase your best content and capture their interest.

d. About section: Craft a compelling and concise channel description in the "About" section. Clearly communicate what your channel is about, the value it provides, and why viewers should subscribe.

e. Social media links: If you have other social media accounts related to your channel, add their links in the "Customize Channel" section. This allows viewers to connect with you on different platforms.

f. Featured sections: Organize your content by creating featured sections on your channel homepage. You can highlight specific playlists, popular videos, or series to guide viewers to your best content.

6. Set up channel branding: In YouTube Studio, navigate to the "Settings" section. Here, you can set up channel branding elements such as watermarks, video thumbnails, and channel defaults. Customize these settings to maintain a consistent visual identity throughout your videos.

7. Enable monetization (optional): If you intend to monetize your channel and earn money from your content, you'll need to meet certain requirements and apply for the YouTube Partner Program. Visit the "Monetization" section in YouTube Studio to learn more about the eligibility criteria and monetization features.

8. Start uploading videos: With your YouTube channel set up, it's time to start uploading your videos. Click on the "Upload" button in the top-right corner of YouTube Studio to begin the uploading process. Follow the prompts to select your video file, add a title, description, tags, and

choose a thumbnail. Be sure to optimize your video settings and metadata to enhance discoverability.

Congratulations! You've successfully set up your YouTube channel. Now, it's time to start creating and sharing your valuable content with the world. Remember to maintain consistency in your branding, engage with your audience through comments and community features, and continually refine your content strategy based on audience feedback and analytics data. Enjoy the journey of building a successful YouTube channel!

CHANNEL ART AND BRANDING

Channel art and branding play a significant role in attracting viewers and establishing a strong visual identity for your YouTube channel. Follow these steps to create compelling channel art and establish a cohesive branding strategy:

1. Designing Channel Art: a. Dimensions and guidelines: The recommended size for channel art is 2560 x 1440 pixels, with a maximum file size of 6MB. Ensure that your artwork is within these dimensions to avoid cropping or distortion. Use image editing software like Adobe Photoshop or Canva to create your channel art.

b. Showcase your brand: Channel art should visually communicate your channel's theme, content, and personality. Consider incorporating your logo, tagline, or elements that represent your niche. Use colors, typography, and imagery that align with your brand and create a strong visual impact.

c. Use high-resolution images: To ensure a crisp and professional look, use high-resolution images or vector graphics. Avoid pixelated or blurry artwork, as it can negatively impact the overall impression of your channel.

d. Consider mobile and TV display: Keep in mind that channel art may appear differently on various devices, such as mobile phones and smart TVs. Test your channel art across different screen sizes to ensure it looks appealing and readable on all platforms.

e. Update seasonally or for special events: Consider updating your channel art to reflect seasonal themes or promote special events or campaigns. This shows your channel is active and engaged with current trends and occasions.

2. Creating a Logo: a. Simple and recognizable: Design a logo that is simple, clean, and easily recognizable. It should be scalable, so it looks good at different sizes. Avoid using too many details or complex graphics that may become unclear when resized.

b. Reflect your brand identity: Your logo should visually represent your channel's theme, values, and personality. It should be aligned with your overall branding strategy and create a cohesive visual identity across your channel and other online platforms.

c. Typography and color choice: Select appropriate typography and colors that complement your brand and convey the right emotions or message. Ensure the logo is legible and visually appealing in various contexts.

d. Professional design assistance: If you lack design skills, consider hiring a professional graphic designer or using online logo design tools to create a high-quality and unique logo for your channel.

3. Consistent Branding: a. Thumbnail templates: Create a consistent visual style for your video thumbnails. Use templates that incorporate your branding elements, fonts, and colors. Consistency in thumbnails helps viewers recognize your content and builds trust.

b. Intro and outro: Create an engaging intro and outro for your videos. Incorporate your logo, channel name, and branding elements to create a cohesive visual experience for viewers. Consistency in intros and outros helps reinforce your brand and improves video recall.

c. Color palette and typography: Establish a consistent color palette and typography across your channel. Use these elements in your channel art, video thumbnails, lower thirds, and other graphic overlays. Consistency in colors and typography helps create a recognizable and professional brand image.

d. Voice and tone: Develop a consistent voice and tone in your videos that aligns with your brand. Whether you're informative, entertaining, or humorous, ensure your content reflects your brand personality consistently.

Remember, channel art and branding should reflect your channel's unique identity and appeal to your target audience. Regularly assess your branding strategy to ensure it remains relevant and resonates with your viewers. By maintaining a visually appealing and cohesive brand presence, you'll enhance your channel's professionalism, recognition, and viewer engagement.

OPTIMIZING CHANNEL SETTINGS AND DESCRIPTION

Optimizing your channel settings and description is essential for attracting viewers, improving discoverability, and providing important information about your YouTube channel. Follow these steps to optimize your channel settings and create a compelling channel description:

1. Channel Settings: a. Channel visibility: In your YouTube Studio, navigate to the "Settings" section and click on the "Channel" tab. Ensure that your channel visibility is set to "Public" so that it can be discovered by viewers.

b. Channel keywords: Select relevant keywords that describe your channel's content and niche. These keywords help YouTube understand the focus of your channel and improve its visibility in search results.

c. Channel country and language: Specify the country and language that best represent your channel. This information helps YouTube recommend your channel to viewers who are interested in content from your region or in your language.

d. Advanced channel settings: Explore the advanced settings options to customize your channel further. This includes options such as channel recommendations, branding watermark, and community contributions.

2. Channel Description: a. Introduction and value proposition: Start your channel description with a compelling introduction that captures viewers' attention. Clearly communicate what your channel is about, the value it provides, and what viewers can expect from your content. Highlight what makes your channel unique and why viewers should subscribe.

b. Relevant links: Include links to your website, blog, social media profiles, and any other platforms where viewers can connect with you. This allows you to build a comprehensive online presence and engage with your audience beyond YouTube.

c. Contact information: Provide contact information such as an email address or business inquiries link for viewers, potential collaborators, or brands interested in reaching out to you. Make it easy for others to contact you for partnership opportunities or inquiries.

d. Social proof: Showcase any notable achievements, awards, or collaborations you have had. This establishes credibility and builds trust with potential viewers.

e. Call-to-action: Encourage viewers to subscribe to your channel and turn on notifications to stay updated with your latest content. You can also invite them to engage with your videos by liking, commenting, and sharing.

f. Timestamps for sections: If your channel has different series, playlists, or recurring segments, consider providing timestamps in the channel description. This allows viewers to easily navigate to specific sections of interest.

3. Channel trailer (optional): a. Engaging and concise: Consider creating a channel trailer—a short video that introduces new viewers to your channel. Make it engaging, exciting, and reflective of the type of content you create. Keep it concise, typically under two minutes, to maintain viewer interest.

b. Show your best content: Feature snippets of your most popular or representative videos in the trailer. This gives viewers a taste of your content and encourages them to explore further.

c. Call-to-action: Include a clear call-to-action at the end of your channel trailer, inviting viewers to subscribe to your channel and explore your content.

Regularly review and update your channel description as your content and channel evolve. Consider testing different descriptions to see which ones resonate best with your audience. By optimizing your channel settings and description, you'll improve your channel's visibility, convey important information to viewers, and increase your chances of attracting subscribers and engagement.

Chapter 4

CONTENT CREATION STRATEGIES

Having created your YouTube channel, it is time to go give the world (your audience) what you've got. If this is your first time you may probably be nervous, not to worry this guide has got it covered. We will discuss in details how to plan your content and how to create compelling videos, taking you by the hand through the whole process. Next, we will look into the filming equipment and software you need to creatively edit and enhance your videos and how to go about it.

Planning Your Content

Planning your content is crucial for maintaining consistency, engaging your audience, and achieving your YouTube channel's goals. By strategizing your content in advance, you can ensure a steady stream of quality videos that resonate with your viewers. Here are steps to effectively plan your content:

1. Define your channel's goals: Start by clarifying the purpose of your YouTube channel. What do you want to achieve? Whether it's educating, entertaining, inspiring, or a combination of these, clearly identify your channel's goals. This will help guide your content planning and ensure your videos align with your overall vision.

2. Know your target audience: Understand who your target audience is and what they are looking for.

Conduct audience research to gather insights about their demographics, interests, preferences, and pain points. This knowledge will enable you to create content that resonates with your viewers and keeps them engaged.

3. Brainstorm content ideas: Set aside dedicated time for brainstorming content ideas. Consider your channel's niche, your expertise, and your audience's interests. Think about different formats, such as tutorials, reviews, vlogs, challenges, or interviews. Use mind mapping techniques, create a content calendar, or maintain a running list of ideas to refer to when planning your videos.

4. Develop a content calendar: A content calendar helps you stay organized and ensures a consistent flow of content. Decide on the frequency of your uploads—whether it's daily, weekly, or monthly—and plan your video topics accordingly. Map out a schedule for filming, editing, and publishing each video. This allows you to plan ahead, maintain a consistent posting schedule, and avoid last-minute rushes.

5. Consider evergreen and trending topics: While evergreen content provides long-term value and remains relevant over time, incorporating trending topics can help attract new viewers and capitalize on current interests. Strike a balance between both types of content to maintain a healthy mix and cater to different viewer needs.

6. Create video series or themes: Developing video series or recurring themes adds structure to your content and keeps viewers coming back for more. It could be a tutorial series, a Q&A segment, a behind-the-scenes look, or a monthly favorites video. Consistency in your series or themes helps build anticipation and loyalty among your audience.

7. Incorporate audience feedback: Pay attention to your viewers' comments, suggestions, and requests. Engage with your audience through comments, community posts, or social media to gather feedback on your existing content and gather ideas for future videos. Incorporating audience feedback makes your viewers feel heard and valued, fostering a strong community around your channel.

8. Experiment and iterate: Don't be afraid to try new things and experiment with different types of content. Test out different formats, styles, or topics to see what resonates best with your audience. Analyze your video analytics to understand which videos perform well and use those insights to refine your content strategy.

Remember, planning your content is an ongoing process. Regularly assess your video performance, stay informed about industry trends, and adapt your content strategy accordingly. By planning your content effectively, you'll create a consistent and engaging experience for your viewers, drive subscriber growth, and build a successful YouTube channel.

CREATING COMPELLING VIDEOS

Creating compelling videos is essential for capturing viewers' attention, keeping them engaged, and encouraging them to subscribe and share your content. Here are some key steps to create videos that stand out:

1. Plan your video structure: Start by outlining the structure of your video. A well-structured video keeps viewers engaged and helps convey your message effectively. Consider using the following elements:

a. Introduction: Hook viewers from the start by introducing the topic or problem you'll address in the video. Create intrigue and establish the value they'll gain from watching.

b. Main content: Present your information, ideas, or story in a clear and organized manner. Break down complex topics into easily digestible segments, and provide examples, visuals, or demonstrations to enhance understanding.

c. Call-to-action: End your video with a strong call-to-action, encouraging viewers to take a specific action such as subscribing, liking, commenting, or sharing. Clearly communicate the benefit of engaging with your channel.

2. Engage visually and audibly: a. Visual quality: Invest in good-quality camera equipment and lighting to ensure clear and visually appealing footage. Consider using a tripod or stabilization techniques for steady shots. Experiment with

different angles, compositions, and visuals to keep the video visually interesting.

b. Audio quality: Use a good-quality microphone to ensure clear and crisp audio. Poor audio quality can be a major turn-off for viewers, so invest in a microphone that suits your recording setup.

c. Editing: Pay attention to editing your videos. Use video editing software to trim unnecessary footage, add transitions, overlays, and effects, and enhance the overall visual experience. Ensure a good pace and flow to keep viewers engaged.

3. Capture attention with thumbnails and titles: a. Thumbnails: Create eye-catching and click-worthy thumbnails that accurately represent the content of your video. Use high-quality images, vibrant colors, and clear text overlays to grab viewers' attention. Test different thumbnail designs and analyze their performance to identify what works best for your channel.

b. Titles: Craft compelling and descriptive titles that accurately represent the content of your video. Use keywords and phrases that are relevant to your niche and appeal to your target audience. A well-crafted title can significantly impact the click-through rate of your videos.

4. Show your personality and passion: a. Be authentic: Let your personality shine through in your videos. Be yourself, and don't be afraid to show your enthusiasm and passion for your content. Viewers appreciate authenticity and are

more likely to connect with creators who are genuine.

b. Engage with your audience: Encourage interaction with your viewers by asking questions, inviting comments, and responding to them. Build a sense of community by acknowledging your audience's contributions and making them feel valued.

5. Deliver value and solve problems: a. Know your audience's needs: Understand the challenges, questions, and pain points of your target audience. Create videos that provide value, solve problems, and offer practical advice or insights. Focus on helping your viewers and addressing their needs.

b. Provide clear takeaways: Ensure that each video delivers clear takeaways or actionable tips that viewers can apply in their own lives. Make it easy for them to understand and implement the information you provide.

6. Continuously improve: a. Analyze video performance: Regularly review your video analytics to gain insights into viewer engagement, watch time, and audience retention. Identify patterns or trends that can inform your content strategy and help you produce more compelling videos.

b. Learn from feedback: Listen to your viewers' feedback and comments. Take constructive criticism positively and make adjustments to enhance your future videos. Engage with your audience to understand their preferences and expectations.

Creating compelling videos takes time and practice. Don't be discouraged if your early videos don't meet your expectations. Keep experimenting, learning, and refining your skills. With each video, strive to improve the quality, engagement, and value you provide to your viewers.

FILMING EQUIPMENT AND SOFTWARE

Having the right filming equipment and software is crucial for producing high-quality videos. While you don't need the most expensive gear to start, investing in some essential equipment can significantly improve the visual and audio aspects of your videos. Here are some key items to consider:

1. Camera:

    - DSLR or Mirrorless Camera: These cameras offer excellent image quality, manual control options, and interchangeable lenses. Popular models include the Canon EOS series, Nikon D series, and Sony Alpha series.

    - Smartphone Camera: Modern smartphones often have impressive camera capabilities, making them a convenient and cost-effective option, especially for vlogging or on-the-go shooting. Make sure to use good lighting and stabilization techniques for optimal results.

2. Tripod or Gimbal:

- Tripod: A tripod provides stability and eliminates shaky footage. Look for a sturdy tripod that suits your camera's weight and offers adjustable height and angles.

- Gimbal: For smooth and professional-looking footage, consider using a gimbal. Gimbals stabilize the camera while you're on the move, resulting in fluid and cinematic shots.

3. Lighting:

  - Natural Light: Take advantage of natural light whenever possible. Position yourself or your subject near a window or shoot outdoors during the golden hours (early morning or late afternoon) for soft and flattering lighting.

  - Studio Lights: If you need consistent lighting indoors or want to control the lighting environment, invest in studio lights. Softbox lights or LED panels are popular options that provide adjustable brightness and color temperature.

4. Microphone:

  - External Microphone: Built-in camera microphones often pick up unwanted background noise. Consider using an external microphone for clear and professional audio. Options include shotgun microphones, lavalier microphones, and USB microphones.

- Audio Recorder: If you need higher audio quality or want more control over audio settings, consider using a separate audio recorder. This allows you to capture audio independently and sync it with your video during editing.

5. Video Editing Software:

- Adobe Premiere Pro: A powerful and widely-used video editing software with advanced features and flexibility.

- Final Cut Pro: A popular choice among Mac users, offering professional editing tools and seamless integration with Apple's ecosystem.

- DaVinci Resolve: A free option with comprehensive editing capabilities, color grading tools, and visual effects.

- iMovie (Mac) and Windows Movie Maker (Windows): Basic editing software pre-installed on respective operating systems, suitable for beginners.

6. Additional Accessories:

- External Hard Drive: As you produce more videos, you'll need additional storage for your raw footage and edited projects. Invest in a reliable external hard drive to keep your files organized and secure.

- Memory Cards: Ensure you have sufficient memory cards with ample storage capacity and fast write speeds to handle high-definition video recording.

- Green Screen: If you plan to create video effects or add virtual backgrounds, a green screen can be a valuable tool. It allows you to replace the green background with different visuals during the editing process.

Remember, the equipment you choose should align with your budget, content requirements, and technical proficiency. As you gain experience and your channel grows, you can gradually upgrade your gear to further enhance the quality of your videos. Additionally, familiarize yourself with the features and capabilities of your chosen software to maximize your editing efficiency and creative options.

EDITING AND ENHANCING YOUR VIDEOS

Editing and enhancing your videos is a crucial step in the production process that allows you to polish your content, add visual flair, and create a professional final product. Here are some key steps to help you edit and enhance your videos effectively:

1. Organize your footage: Before you begin editing, ensure that your video files are well-organized. Create a dedicated folder for each project and sort your footage into categorized folders, making it easier to locate specific clips during the editing process.

2. Choose the right video editing software: Select a video editing software that suits your needs and level of expertise. Popular options include Adobe Premiere Pro, Final Cut Pro, DaVinci Resolve, iMovie, and Windows Movie Maker. Explore the features and capabilities of your chosen software to maximize its potential.

3. Trim and arrange your clips: Start by importing your video footage into the editing software's timeline. Review each clip and remove any unnecessary or unwanted sections. Arrange the remaining clips in the desired order to create a cohesive narrative or flow.

4. Add transitions: Smoothly transition between clips by adding transitions. Popular transition options include cuts, fades, dissolves, wipes, and slides. Use transitions sparingly and purposefully to maintain visual interest without overwhelming the viewer.

5. Enhance the visual quality:

   - Color correction: Adjust the color balance, exposure, contrast, saturation, and other parameters to achieve a visually pleasing look. Ensure consistency in color and lighting throughout the video.

   - Filters and effects: Experiment with filters, effects, and overlays to enhance the visual style or mood of your video. However, use them judiciously to avoid distracting or overpowering the content.

- Text and graphics: Include text overlays, lower thirds, or graphics to provide additional information, context, or branding. Use readable fonts, appropriate sizes, and suitable colors to ensure clarity.

6. Incorporate audio elements:

    - Background music: Choose appropriate background music that complements the tone and style of your video. Ensure that the music enhances the viewer's experience without overpowering dialogue or narration.

    - Sound effects: Consider adding sound effects to emphasize actions, enhance storytelling, or create a more immersive experience. Use them subtly and purposefully to avoid overwhelming the audio mix.

    - Voiceover or narration: If needed, record a voiceover or narration to provide additional context or explanation. Ensure clear and high-quality audio recording, and synchronize it with the appropriate visuals.

7. Cutaways and B-roll footage: To add visual interest and provide context, incorporate cutaway shots or B-roll footage. These additional clips can be overlaid or inserted at appropriate moments to support or enhance the main content.

8. Apply video and audio effects: Experiment with video and audio effects, such as slow motion, fast

motion, stabilization, or audio filters, to add creative elements or correct technical issues. However, exercise restraint and use effects purposefully to avoid detracting from the overall quality and message of your video.

9. Optimize audio levels: Ensure that the audio levels are balanced and consistent throughout the video. Adjust the volume, normalize audio peaks, and reduce background noise or distractions as necessary. Aim for clear and intelligible audio.

10. Preview and refine: Regularly preview your edited video to ensure smooth transitions, coherent storytelling, and visual appeal. Make necessary adjustments, fine-tune edits, and address any issues or inconsistencies that may arise during the review process.

11. Export and save: Once you're satisfied with your edited video, export it in the appropriate format and resolution. Consider optimizing the file size without sacrificing quality to facilitate faster uploading and streaming. Save a backup of your edited project file for future reference or re-editing if needed.

Remember, editing is a skill that improves with practice and experimentation. Take the time to explore various editing techniques, study tutorials, and analyze videos from successful YouTubers to gain inspiration and insights. With each video you edit, strive for a polished, engaging, and visually appealing final product that aligns with your channel's brand and content.

OPTIMIZING VIDEO TITLES, DESCRIPTIONS, AND TAGS

Optimizing your video titles, descriptions, and tags is crucial for increasing your video's visibility, discoverability, and ranking on YouTube's search results. By incorporating relevant keywords and providing accurate and engaging information, you can attract more viewers and grow your audience. Here are some key strategies for optimizing these elements:

1. Video Titles:

    - Be descriptive and concise: Craft titles that accurately reflect the content of your video and capture viewers' attention. Include important keywords early in the title to improve search visibility.

    - Highlight the value: Communicate the benefit or value that viewers will gain from watching your video. Make it clear what problem you're addressing or what information you're providing.

    - Use engaging language: Incorporate compelling and action-oriented words that pique viewers' curiosity or emotions. Experiment with different approaches to find what resonates with your audience.

2. Video Descriptions:

    - Include a detailed summary: Provide a comprehensive and informative description of your video. Summarize the main points, key takeaways, or highlights.

- Utilize keywords: Incorporate relevant keywords naturally throughout the description to improve search rankings. However, avoid keyword stuffing, as it can negatively impact your video's visibility.

- Add timestamps: If your video covers different topics or segments, include timestamps in the description. This allows viewers to navigate directly to specific sections of interest, enhancing the user experience.

- Include relevant links: Add links to your website, social media profiles, or related resources mentioned in the video. This helps drive traffic and engagement beyond YouTube.

3. Video Tags:

- Use relevant and specific tags: Include tags that accurately represent the content, topic, and keywords associated with your video. Choose a mix of broad and specific tags to target different search queries.

- Research popular tags: Analyze tags used by popular and relevant videos in your niche. Incorporate similar tags that align with your video's content to increase the chances of appearing in related search results.

- Optimize for long-tail keywords: Consider using long-tail keywords as tags, as they have less competition and can attract more targeted viewers. Long-tail keywords are longer, more specific phrases rather than generic terms.

- Tag variations and synonyms: Use variations or synonyms of your main keywords as tags. This broadens the scope of your video's relevance and can capture viewers searching with different terms.

4. Thumbnail optimization:

- Create eye-catching thumbnails: Design visually appealing thumbnails that accurately represent your video's content and entice viewers to click. Use high-quality images, vibrant colors, and clear text overlays.

- Maintain consistency: Establish a consistent thumbnail style or branding for your channel. This helps viewers recognize your videos and builds trust and credibility.

5. Additional tips:

- Monitor analytics: Regularly review your video analytics to gain insights into search traffic, click-through rates, and viewer engagement. Adjust your titles, descriptions, and tags based on the performance data to optimize future videos.

- Stay up to date: Keep abreast of YouTube's algorithm updates and changes in search trends. Adjust your optimization strategies accordingly to stay competitive and maintain visibility.

Remember, while optimizing your titles, descriptions, and tags is essential, it's equally important to create high-quality, engaging content that delivers value to your viewers. Strive for a balance between optimization techniques and providing a meaningful and enjoyable viewing experience.

Chapter 5

BUILDING AN ENGAGED COMMUNITY

As a content creator, it is not just about producing great videos; it is about fostering a sense of belonging, interaction, and loyalty among your viewers. An engaged community is the lifeblood of any YouTube channel, as it creates a space where your viewers can connect, interact, and feel a genuine sense of involvement with your content. It is within this community that relationships are formed, discussions flourish, and a strong support network emerges. Building such a community takes time, effort, and a deep understanding of your audience's needs and desires.

Understanding the Importance of Community

Building a strong community on YouTube is essential for the success and growth of your channel. Your community consists of your subscribers, viewers, and engaged fans who support and interact with your content. Understanding the importance of community and actively nurturing it can have numerous benefits for your channel. Here's why community matters:

1. Fosters engagement and interaction: A thriving community encourages viewers to actively engage with your videos through likes, comments, and shares. It creates a sense of connection and dialogue between you and your audience, fostering a deeper level of engagement and interaction.

2. Builds loyalty and trust: When you cultivate a supportive community, viewers are more likely to develop loyalty towards your channel. They become invested in your content and brand, regularly returning for new videos and recommending your channel to others. Building trust within your community establishes your credibility and strengthens your influence.

3. Provides valuable feedback and ideas: Your community can serve as a valuable source of feedback, ideas, and suggestions. Pay attention to the comments and messages you receive, as they can provide insights into what your audience enjoys, what they want to see more of, and areas for improvement. Engage in conversations with your community to foster a collaborative and inclusive environment.

4. Creates a sense of belonging: Being part of a community gives viewers a sense of belonging and connection. By actively responding to comments, acknowledging your audience, and creating opportunities for them to engage with each other, you foster a supportive and inclusive atmosphere where viewers feel valued and included.

5. Amplifies your reach and exposure: A strong community can become your biggest advocates, sharing your videos with their own networks and helping to expand your reach. Word-of-mouth recommendations from engaged community members can significantly boost your channel's exposure and attract new viewers.

6. Encourages collaboration and partnerships: As your community grows, you may have opportunities to collaborate with other YouTubers or industry professionals. These collaborations can introduce your channel to new audiences, provide fresh content ideas, and establish beneficial partnerships that mutually benefit all parties involved.

7. Drives channel growth and success: A supportive and engaged community is more likely to help your channel grow in terms of subscribers, views, and overall success. Their active participation in liking, sharing, and commenting on your videos can improve your video's visibility and performance in search and recommendation algorithms.

To foster a thriving community:

- Respond to comments: Engage with your viewers by replying to comments and showing genuine interest in their thoughts and opinions.

- Create community-centric content: Encourage discussions and feedback by creating videos that directly involve and address your community's interests and questions.

- Host live streams and Q&A sessions: Interact with your community in real-time through live streams and Q&A sessions, allowing for direct conversation and connection.

- Participate in social media platforms: Extend your community-building efforts beyond YouTube by actively engaging with your audience on social media platforms like Twitter, Instagram, and Facebook.

- Establish community guidelines: Set clear community guidelines that promote respect, inclusivity, and constructive dialogue. Monitor and moderate comments to maintain a positive environment.

Remember, building a strong community takes time and effort. Stay engaged, responsive, and appreciative of your community's support, and continue to provide value through your content and interactions. By nurturing your community, you create a loyal and dedicated audience that will contribute to the long-term success of your YouTube channel.

ENCOURAGING ENGAGEMENT AND INTERACTION

Engagement and interaction are vital aspects of a successful YouTube channel. They not only enhance the viewer experience but also contribute to the growth and visibility of your content. Here are some effective strategies to encourage engagement and interaction with your audience:

1. Pose questions and prompts: Encourage viewers to share their thoughts and opinions by asking questions related to your video's content. Invite them to leave comments with their perspectives, experiences, or suggestions. Make it clear that their input is valued and appreciated.

2. Respond to comments: Actively engage with your audience by responding to their comments. Take the time to acknowledge their feedback, answer their questions, and thank them for their support. This interaction demonstrates that you genuinely care about your viewers' input and encourages further engagement.

3. Foster a sense of community: Create a welcoming and inclusive atmosphere where viewers feel comfortable interacting with each other. Encourage viewers to engage with one another by responding to each other's comments and sharing their own experiences. Highlight interesting or insightful comments in your videos or community posts to showcase viewer participation.

4. Conduct polls and surveys: Use YouTube's poll feature or external survey tools to gather feedback from your audience. Pose questions related to your channel's content, future video ideas, or topics of interest. Sharing the results of these polls or surveys in a subsequent video can spark further discussions and engagement.

5. Incorporate interactive elements in your videos: Integrate interactive elements, such as quizzes, challenges, or games, into your videos to actively involve your viewers. Encourage them to participate and share their results or experiences in the comments section. This not only boosts engagement but also adds an element of fun and interactivity to your content.

6. Host live streams and Q&A sessions: Schedule live streams or dedicated Q&A sessions where you can interact with your audience in real-time. Allow viewers to ask questions, provide feedback, and engage in live chat discussions. This direct interaction creates a sense of connection and makes viewers feel involved in your channel's community.

7. Create video series or collaborations featuring viewers: Consider featuring your viewers in your videos by showcasing their content, reactions, or testimonials. This collaborative approach makes viewers feel valued and encourages them to actively contribute to your channel.

8. Use call-to-action (CTA) overlays and end screens: Prompt viewers to engage further by using CTA overlays or end screens in your videos. Encourage them to like, comment, share, or subscribe to your channel. Make it easy for them to take action by providing clear instructions and clickable links.

9. Engage on social media platforms: Extend your engagement efforts beyond YouTube by actively participating on social media platforms where your audience is present. Respond to comments, messages, and mentions on platforms like Twitter, Instagram, or Facebook. This multi-channel interaction strengthens your relationship with your audience and expands your reach.

10. Reward and recognize engagement: Show appreciation for your viewers' engagement by

acknowledging and rewarding their contributions. Give shoutouts to active and engaged community members in your videos or community posts. Consider hosting giveaways, contests, or exclusive perks for your most dedicated supporters.

Remember, consistent and meaningful engagement fosters a loyal and dedicated community. Take the time to understand your audience, listen to their feedback, and create content that resonates with them. By actively encouraging and valuing their engagement, you can create a thriving and interactive YouTube community.

RESPONDING TO COMMENTS AND FEEDBACK

Responding to comments and feedback is a crucial aspect of building a strong and engaged community on YouTube. By actively engaging with your viewers, you create a sense of connection and appreciation, foster meaningful discussions, and build a loyal fan base. Here are some tips for effectively responding to comments and feedback:

1. Be prompt: Aim to respond to comments in a timely manner, preferably within the first 24-48 hours. This shows your viewers that you value their input and are actively involved in the conversation.

2. Be genuine and authentic: When responding to comments, be sincere and authentic in your interactions. Show gratitude for positive feedback, address concerns or questions with

empathy, and express genuine interest in your viewers' perspectives. Avoid generic or automated responses.

3. Stay positive and respectful: Maintain a positive and respectful tone in your replies, even when addressing negative or critical comments. Responding with kindness and understanding helps to defuse potential conflicts and demonstrates your professionalism.

4. Provide helpful information: When viewers ask questions or seek clarification, strive to provide accurate and helpful information in your responses. Be concise and to the point, offering solutions or additional resources if necessary. Your expertise and willingness to assist will further establish your credibility.

5. Encourage further discussion: Use your responses as an opportunity to stimulate further conversation. Pose follow-up questions, seek additional input, or invite viewers to share their own experiences or opinions. This encourages engagement and fosters a sense of community.

6. Address constructive criticism: Constructive criticism can provide valuable insights and opportunities for growth. When receiving feedback, take the time to understand the viewer's perspective and respond in a receptive manner. Thank them for their input and explain any steps you may take to address their concerns.

7. Moderate comments appropriately: Maintain a respectful and inclusive comment section by moderating inappropriate or spam comments. Encourage healthy discussions while discouraging offensive or disrespectful behavior. Set clear community guidelines to provide a framework for acceptable behavior.

8. Consider creating dedicated comment response videos: If you receive numerous comments or have common themes emerging, consider creating a dedicated video where you address and respond to specific comments or feedback. This allows you to engage with your audience on a broader scale and encourages viewers to continue the conversation.

9. Monitor feedback across platforms: In addition to YouTube comments, keep an eye on feedback and comments you receive on other platforms such as social media, email, or community forums. Respond to relevant feedback across all platforms to demonstrate your commitment to engaging with your audience.

10. Learn from feedback: Embrace feedback as an opportunity for growth and improvement. Analyze common feedback themes or suggestions and consider implementing changes or adjustments to your content or channel strategy based on viewer input.

Remember, every interaction with your viewers is an opportunity to build a meaningful connection and strengthen your community. By actively responding to comments and feedback, you show your viewers that their voices are heard and valued. This engagement fosters loyalty, encourages further participation, and contributes to the long-term success of your YouTube channel.

COLLABORATING WITH OTHER YOUTUBERS

Collaborating with other YouTubers is a powerful strategy for expanding your reach, introducing new content to your audience, and building valuable relationships within the YouTube community. By teaming up with like-minded creators, you can tap into their audience, gain exposure to new viewers, and create engaging and unique content. Here are some key steps and considerations for successful collaborations:

1. Identify compatible creators: Look for YouTubers whose content aligns with your niche or complements your own. Consider factors such as audience demographics, content style, and values. Seek out creators with a similar or slightly larger subscriber base to maximize the potential impact of the collaboration.

2. Research and evaluate potential collaborators: Take the time to thoroughly research potential collaborators. Watch their videos, read their comments, and review their engagement levels. Assess the quality of their content, their engagement with their own audience, and their overall reputation within the YouTube community.

3. Establish mutual goals and expectations: Before initiating a collaboration, have open and honest discussions with the other YouTuber to establish shared goals and expectations. Determine the purpose of the collaboration, whether it's to create a joint video, cross-promote each other's channels, or explore other creative opportunities. Align on timelines, content ideas, and the level of commitment required from both parties.

4. Plan the collaboration: Collaborations work best when there is a well-thought-out plan. Discuss and agree upon the theme, format, and content of the collaborative video. Coordinate schedules, logistics, and any necessary equipment or resources. Consider brainstorming together to generate fresh and exciting ideas that will engage both audiences.

5. Leverage each other's strengths: Capitalize on the unique strengths and expertise of each collaborator to create a well-rounded and compelling video. Each YouTuber can bring their own perspectives, knowledge, and style to the collaboration, making it more interesting and valuable for both sets of viewers.

6. Cross-promote and leverage existing audiences: Promote the collaborative video across both channels to leverage each other's existing audiences. Encourage your viewers to check out the other creator's channel and subscribe, and ask your collaborator to do the same. This cross-promotion can introduce new viewers to your content and build long-term connections.

7. Communicate and collaborate effectively: Maintain clear and open communication throughout the collaboration process. Regularly update each other on progress, share feedback, and address any concerns promptly. Establish a shared timeline, deadlines, and milestones to ensure a smooth and efficient collaboration experience.

8. Create engaging and high-quality content: Put in the effort to create content that is engaging, entertaining, and aligned with both collaborators' styles. Aim to provide value to both sets of viewers and create a seamless viewing experience. Ensure that the production quality, editing, and overall presentation meet the standards of both channels.

9. Foster long-term relationships: Collaborations can pave the way for long-term relationships with other YouTubers. Maintain connections beyond the collaboration by supporting each other's content, engaging with their audience, and exploring future opportunities together. This fosters a sense of community and opens doors to further collaborations down the line.

10. Track and evaluate the results: After the collaboration, analyze the performance of the collaborative video. Monitor metrics such as views, engagement, new subscribers, and audience feedback. Assess the impact of the collaboration on your channel's growth and audience reach. Use this information to refine

future collaboration strategies and make informed decisions.

Remember, collaborating with other YouTubers is not only about expanding your reach but also about creating meaningful and valuable content for your audience. Choose collaborators who align with your vision, and approach collaborations with a mindset of mutual support and creativity. By leveraging the strengths and audiences of both collaborators, you can create exciting content that resonates with viewers and strengthens your presence within the YouTube community.

Chapter 6

PROMOTING YOUR YOUTUBE CHANNEL

Promoting your YouTube channel is a crucial step in building a successful online presence. While creating high-quality content is essential, it is equally important to ensure that your content reaches the right audience

UTILIZING SOCIAL MEDIA

Social media platforms are powerful tools for promoting your YouTube channel, engaging with your audience, and expanding your online presence. By strategically utilizing social media, you can reach new viewers, drive traffic to your YouTube videos, and build a strong online community. Here are some effective strategies for leveraging social media to enhance your YouTube channel:

1. Identify the right platforms: Research and identify the social media platforms that are most relevant to your target audience and align with your content. Popular platforms for YouTubers include Instagram, Twitter, Facebook, TikTok, and LinkedIn. Focus your efforts on platforms where your audience is most active.

2. Optimize your profiles: Ensure that your social media profiles are complete, professional, and consistent with your branding. Use high-quality

profile pictures, compelling bio descriptions, and links to your YouTube channel. Optimize keywords and hashtags to make it easier for users to discover your content.

3. Promote your YouTube videos: Share teasers, trailers, or snippets of your YouTube videos on social media to pique the interest of your followers. Include compelling captions, eye-catching thumbnails, and relevant hashtags to increase visibility. Direct viewers to watch the full video on your YouTube channel by providing a link in your post.

4. Engage with your audience: Actively engage with your followers by responding to comments, answering questions, and acknowledging their support. Foster a sense of community by initiating conversations, conducting polls, or sharing behind-the-scenes glimpses. Encourage users to share their thoughts, experiences, and ideas related to your content.

5. Cross-promote with other creators: Collaborate with other YouTubers or social media influencers by featuring each other's content or mentioning one another in posts. This cross-promotion exposes your channel to new audiences and can lead to mutually beneficial partnerships.

6. Utilize hashtags and trends: Stay updated with trending topics, hashtags, and challenges relevant to your niche. Incorporate these trends into your content or join conversations around them. Using popular hashtags helps your content

appear in search results and exposes your channel to a wider audience.

7. Create platform-specific content: Tailor your content to each social media platform's format and audience preferences. For example, create visually appealing images or graphics for Instagram, short and engaging videos for TikTok, or informative threads for Twitter. Adapt your content to optimize engagement and shareability on each platform.

8. Schedule and automate posts: Consistency is key on social media. Create a content calendar and schedule your posts in advance using social media management tools like Hootsuite or Buffer. Automating your posts ensures that you maintain an active presence even during busy periods.

9. Analyze and optimize your performance: Regularly analyze your social media metrics to understand what types of content resonate best with your audience. Monitor engagement, reach, and follower growth. Use these insights to refine your social media strategy and focus on content that generates the most traction.

10. Leverage paid advertising: Consider allocating a budget for targeted social media advertising campaigns to reach a wider audience. Platforms like Facebook and Instagram offer detailed targeting options that allow you to reach specific demographics or interests aligned with your content.

Remember, social media is not just a promotional tool but also a platform for building relationships and connecting with your audience. Be genuine, interactive, and consistent in your social media presence. By effectively utilizing social media, you can amplify your YouTube channel's reach, foster engagement, and establish a strong online brand presence.

CROSS-PROMOTION AND COLLABORATIONS

Cross-promotion and collaborations with other YouTubers are excellent strategies for expanding your reach, attracting new viewers, and fostering a sense of community within the YouTube platform. By teaming up with fellow creators, you can leverage each other's audiences and create mutually beneficial content. Here are some key considerations for successful cross-promotion and collaborations:

1. Find compatible channels: Look for YouTubers whose content aligns with your niche or complements your own. Seek out creators whose audience demographics and interests overlap with yours. Look for channels that share a similar size or slightly larger following to maximize the impact of the collaboration.

2. Establish shared goals: Before initiating a cross-promotion or collaboration, have a clear conversation with the other YouTuber about your shared goals and expectations. Define what you both hope to achieve through the collaboration, whether it's reaching a wider audience,

increasing subscriber count, or creating unique and engaging content.

3. Plan the collaboration: Collaborations work best when there is a well-structured plan in place. Discuss and agree upon the format, theme, and content of the collaborative video or project. Coordinate logistics such as shooting schedules, scriptwriting, and any necessary resources or equipment. Ensure that both parties have a clear understanding of their roles and responsibilities.

4. Create synergy: Leverage each other's strengths and expertise to create engaging and unique content. Identify areas where your skills and knowledge complement each other. This can result in a more diverse and interesting video that appeals to both sets of audiences.

5. Cross-promote on your channels: Promote the collaborative content on both of your channels. Create teaser trailers or behind-the-scenes footage to generate excitement and anticipation. Encourage your viewers to check out the other YouTuber's channel and subscribe. Consider featuring the collaboration prominently in your channel's homepage or video description to increase visibility.

6. Collaborate beyond video content: Explore opportunities to collaborate beyond video content. You can co-host live streams, podcasts, or create joint merchandise or giveaways. These initiatives can deepen the connection between your audiences and foster ongoing engagement.

7. Engage with each other's audiences: When the collaborative content is released, actively engage with the comments and feedback from both channels. Respond to viewers' comments, address their questions, and express gratitude for their support. Engaging with each other's audiences helps build a sense of community and strengthens the bond between your channels.

8. Analyze and assess the results: After the collaboration, analyze the performance of the collaborative content. Monitor metrics such as views, engagement, subscriber growth, and audience feedback. Assess the impact of the collaboration on both channels and identify any areas for improvement. Use these insights to refine future collaborations and maximize their effectiveness.

9. Build long-term relationships: Collaborations can pave the way for long-term relationships with other YouTubers. Stay connected beyond the collaboration by supporting each other's content, collaborating on future projects, or participating in each other's videos. Building these relationships contributes to a supportive and thriving YouTube community.

10. Seek diverse collaborations: Don't limit yourself to collaborations within your immediate niche. Look for opportunities to collaborate with creators from different niches or with unique perspectives. This can introduce your channel to new audiences and provide fresh and exciting content for your viewers.

Remember, cross-promotion and collaborations are mutually beneficial opportunities that can help you expand your reach and engage with new audiences. Approach these collaborations with an open mind, a spirit of collaboration, and a focus on creating valuable and entertaining content for your viewers. By collaborating with other YouTubers, you can accelerate your channel's growth and foster a sense of camaraderie within the YouTube community.

SEARCH ENGINE OPTIMIZATION (SEO) FOR YOUTUBE

Search Engine Optimization (SEO) plays a crucial role in increasing the visibility of your YouTube channel and videos in search results. By optimizing your content with relevant keywords and implementing SEO best practices, you can attract more organic traffic, improve your ranking, and reach a wider audience. Here are some essential strategies for optimizing your YouTube videos for search engines:

1. Keyword research: Conduct thorough keyword research to identify the terms and phrases that your target audience is using to search for content similar to yours. Use keyword research tools like Google Keyword Planner, YouTube Autocomplete, or third-party tools to find popular and relevant keywords. Focus on long-tail keywords that are more specific and have less competition.

2. Title optimization: Craft compelling and keyword-rich titles for your videos. Place the most

important keywords at the beginning of the title to increase their visibility. Keep the title concise, descriptive, and engaging to attract clicks from search results.

3. Description optimization: Write detailed and keyword-rich video descriptions that provide context and information about your content. Include relevant keywords naturally within the description, but avoid keyword stuffing. Use the description to provide a summary of the video, timestamps, links to related resources, and calls to action.

4. Tags optimization: Add relevant tags to your videos to help YouTube understand the content and context of your video. Include both broad and specific tags that are related to your content. Use tags that are popular within your niche, but also consider niche-specific or long-tail tags that have less competition. Avoid using misleading or irrelevant tags.

5. Thumbnail optimization: Create visually appealing and click-worthy thumbnails that accurately represent your video content. Use high-quality images, compelling text overlays, and contrasting colors to grab viewers' attention. Consider featuring human faces or emotions to make the thumbnail more relatable and engaging.

6. Closed captions and subtitles: Provide closed captions or subtitles for your videos to improve accessibility and enhance search visibility. Closed captions also allow search engines to

understand the audio content of your videos, which can contribute to better rankings.

7. Video file optimization: Optimize your video file before uploading it to YouTube. Compress the video file size without compromising the quality to ensure faster loading times. Use a compatible video format and consider using a descriptive filename that includes relevant keywords.

8. Engage viewers with compelling content: The engagement and watch time of your videos are critical factors in YouTube's search ranking algorithm. Create high-quality, engaging, and informative content that captivates viewers and encourages them to watch your videos in their entirety. Retaining viewers and earning likes, comments, and shares can positively impact your search rankings.

9. Encourage user engagement: Actively encourage your viewers to engage with your videos by liking, commenting, and sharing. Respond promptly to comments to foster discussions and increase engagement. Engagement signals are important factors that influence YouTube's search rankings.

10. Promote and share your videos: Share your videos across various online platforms, such as your website, blog, social media accounts, and relevant online communities. The more exposure your videos receive, the higher the chances of attracting organic views and increasing your search visibility.

11. Monitor analytics and adjust your strategy: Regularly analyze your YouTube analytics to understand how your videos are performing. Pay attention to metrics like watch time, audience retention, click-through rate, and audience demographics. Use these insights to refine your SEO strategy, identify successful content types, and make data-driven decisions.

Remember, search engine optimization for YouTube is an ongoing process. Continuously monitor and optimize your videos to adapt to changing algorithms, trends, and audience preferences. By implementing effective SEO strategies, you can improve your YouTube channel's visibility, attract more organic traffic, and grow your subscriber base.

PROMOTING YOUR VIDEOS OUTSIDE OF YOUTUBE

While YouTube is a powerful platform for sharing your videos, promoting them outside of YouTube can help expand your reach, attract new viewers, and drive traffic to your channel. Here are some effective strategies for promoting your YouTube videos beyond the platform:

1. Share on social media: Leverage your presence on social media platforms such as Facebook, Twitter, Instagram, LinkedIn, and TikTok to share your YouTube videos. Craft compelling captions, use eye-catching thumbnails, and include relevant hashtags to increase visibility. Encourage your followers to watch the full video

by providing a direct link to your YouTube channel or the specific video.

2. Embed on your website or blog: If you have a website or blog, embed your YouTube videos within relevant articles or pages. This allows visitors to watch your videos directly on your website, increasing engagement and keeping users on your site for longer periods. Additionally, optimize your website or blog for search engines to attract organic traffic to your video pages.

3. Collaborate with influencers: Identify influencers or content creators in your niche who have a substantial following and collaborate with them. Whether it's through a sponsored video, a guest appearance, or a shoutout, leveraging the influence of others can introduce your channel to a wider audience and generate new subscribers.

4. Guest post on blogs or websites: Reach out to popular blogs or websites within your niche and offer to create guest posts or contribute articles related to your video content. Include relevant links to your YouTube videos within the articles to drive traffic back to your channel. Guest posting can expose your content to new audiences and establish your credibility as a knowledgeable creator.

5. Participate in online communities: Engage with online communities, forums, and discussion boards related to your niche. Provide valuable insights, answer questions, and share your expertise. When appropriate, mention or link to

your YouTube videos as a resource or reference. However, ensure you follow community guidelines and avoid spamming or self-promotion.

6. Email marketing: If you have an email list or newsletter, regularly promote your latest YouTube videos to your subscribers. Craft compelling subject lines and include a brief description or teaser of the video within the email. Directly link to the video or your YouTube channel to drive clicks and views.

7. Utilize cross-platform promotion: If you have a presence on other platforms such as Twitch, podcasts, or streaming services, promote your YouTube videos to your audience on those platforms. Cross-promotion allows you to reach viewers who may not be aware of your YouTube channel and can help drive traffic and subscribers.

8. Run paid advertising campaigns: Consider allocating a budget for paid advertising campaigns on platforms like Google Ads, social media platforms, or YouTube's own advertising options. With targeted advertising, you can reach specific demographics or interests aligned with your content, driving relevant traffic to your YouTube videos.

9. Engage with online influencers and communities: Actively engage with influencers, thought leaders, and communities in your niche. Leave thoughtful comments on their content, share their

videos, and participate in discussions. Building genuine relationships can lead to organic shoutouts, collaborations, or recommendations that expose your channel to a wider audience.

10. Utilize SEO and video optimization: Implement search engine optimization (SEO) techniques within your video titles, descriptions, tags, and thumbnails to increase your video's discoverability in search engines like Google. Optimized videos have a higher chance of appearing in search results and attracting organic traffic.

Remember, promoting your YouTube videos outside of the platform requires consistent effort and strategic planning. Experiment with different promotional strategies to identify what works best for your channel and target audience. By diversifying your promotional efforts, you can increase your channel's visibility, attract new viewers, and ultimately grow your YouTube presence.

Chapter 7

MONETIZATION STRATEGIES

As a content creator, it is natural to aspire to turn your passion into a sustainable source of income. In this chapter, we will explore the various avenues available to monetize your YouTube channel, empowering you to maximize your earning potential while providing value to your audience. Monetizing your YouTube channel goes beyond simply creating and uploading videos. It involves understanding the platforms' policies, discovering different revenue streams, and strategically leveraging your content and audience to generate income. Walk through the guide below to absorb the essential monetization strategies that can help you transform your channel into a profitable venture.

YOUTUBE PARTNER PROGRAM AND AD REVENUE

The YouTube Partner Program (YPP) is an opportunity for creators to monetize their content and earn ad revenue on YouTube. Once you meet the program's eligibility requirements and join, you can start generating income from the ads that appear on your videos. Here's an overview of the YouTube Partner Program and how ad revenue works:

1. Eligibility requirements: To join the YouTube Partner Program, you need to meet certain

criteria. These requirements typically include having at least 1,000 subscribers on your channel and accumulating a minimum of 4,000 watch hours in the past 12 months. Additionally, you must comply with YouTube's policies and guidelines, including copyright and community guidelines.

2. Applying for the program: Once you meet the eligibility criteria, you can apply for the YouTube Partner Program through your YouTube Studio. The application process involves providing necessary information, agreeing to the terms and conditions, and reviewing your channel for compliance with YouTube's policies.

3. Monetization options: Once accepted into the YouTube Partner Program, you gain access to various monetization options:

a. Ad revenue: The primary way to earn income is through ads displayed on your videos. YouTube's automated systems place relevant ads based on factors like viewer demographics, content type, and advertiser preferences.

b. Channel memberships: Eligible channels can offer channel memberships to their subscribers, allowing them to pay a monthly fee to access exclusive perks and content.

c. Super Chat and Super Stickers: If you engage with your audience through live streams, Super Chat allows viewers to purchase chat messages that are highlighted during the stream. Super Stickers are animated stickers that viewers can purchase to support creators during live chats.

d. YouTube Premium revenue: When YouTube Premium subscribers watch your videos, you receive a portion of the revenue generated by their subscription fees.

4. Ad formats: YouTube offers various ad formats that can appear on your videos:

a. Display ads: These are overlay ads that appear on the lower portion of the video while it's playing.

b. Skippable video ads: These ads allow viewers to skip after a few seconds, but you still earn revenue if they watch a certain duration of the ad.

c. Non-skippable video ads: These ads must be watched in their entirety before the viewer can access your video.

d. Sponsored cards: These are small, clickable cards that appear within your video, showcasing sponsored content or products.

e. Mid-roll ads: These are ads that play during longer videos, typically after the viewer has watched a significant portion of the video.

5. Ad revenue calculation: YouTube shares a portion of the ad revenue with creators. The exact revenue share percentage can vary, but generally, creators receive around 55% of the ad revenue, while YouTube retains the remaining 45%.

6. Factors influencing ad revenue: Several factors affect the amount of ad revenue you can generate:

a. Video views and watch time: The more views and watch time your videos accumulate, the higher your potential ad revenue.

b. Advertiser demand: The availability and competition among advertisers for ad placements can impact ad rates and overall revenue.

c. Audience demographics: Advertisers may target specific demographics, so if your audience aligns with their target market, you may attract higher-paying ads.

d. Content relevance and quality: Creating valuable, high-quality content that resonates with your audience can result in better viewer engagement and higher ad revenue.

7. Payment and threshold: Once you start earning ad revenue, you'll accumulate earnings in your AdSense account linked to your YouTube channel. When your earnings reach the payment threshold, typically set at $100, you can request a payment. Payments are typically made through direct deposit or other available payment methods in your region.

Remember, while ad revenue is an essential part of monetizing your YouTube channel, it's not the only way to generate income. Many creators also explore additional revenue streams such as brand sponsorships, merchandise sales, crowdfunding, and affiliate marketing. Diversifying your income sources can provide stability and further financial opportunities as you grow your YouTube channel.

SPONSORSHIPS AND BRAND DEALS

Sponsorships and brand deals are lucrative opportunities for YouTubers to generate income and collaborate with brands. By partnering with companies relevant to your content and audience, you can not only earn money but also enhance your channel's credibility and reach. Here's an overview of sponsorships and brand deals and how you can secure them:

1. What are sponsorships and brand deals? Sponsorships and brand deals involve collaborating with companies or brands that align with your content niche or target audience. Brands may sponsor your videos or channels by providing financial support, products, or services in exchange for promotion and exposure to your audience.

2. Building your brand and audience: To attract sponsorships, focus on building a strong brand and growing your audience. Create high-quality, engaging content that resonates with your target audience and showcases your expertise in your niche. Consistently engage with your viewers, foster a loyal community, and demonstrate your influence and credibility.

3. Identifying potential sponsors: Research and identify brands that align with your content and target audience. Look for companies that have an

active presence on YouTube or have sponsored other creators in your niche. Consider the relevance of their products or services to your content and audience's interests.

4. Reaching out to brands: Once you've identified potential sponsors, you can reach out to them directly or through influencer marketing platforms. Craft a professional and personalized pitch that highlights the value you can provide to the brand. Showcase your channel's demographics, engagement metrics, and past successful collaborations, if any. Emphasize how partnering with you can benefit their brand and reach their target audience.

5. Negotiating sponsorship terms: When discussing sponsorship terms, consider factors such as the duration of the partnership, the number and type of sponsored videos, exclusivity agreements, and the compensation or benefits you'll receive. Be open to negotiation but ensure the terms align with your channel's values and audience's interests.

6. Disclosing sponsorships: Transparency is essential when collaborating with brands. Comply with YouTube's guidelines and disclose any sponsored content or brand deals clearly to your audience. This can be done through verbal disclosures in your videos, including written disclaimers in the video description, or using YouTube's built-in disclosure features.

7. Creating sponsored content: When creating sponsored videos, maintain authenticity and ensure the content integrates seamlessly with your usual content style. Focus on providing value to your audience and showcasing the brand's products or services in an engaging and informative manner. Strive to strike a balance between promotion and maintaining the trust of your viewers.

8. Evaluating brand fit and credibility: Before entering into sponsorships or brand deals, carefully evaluate the brand's fit with your channel and your audience's needs. Ensure the brand's values align with yours and that their products or services are of high quality and relevance to your viewers. Collaborating with reputable brands enhances your channel's credibility and maintains trust with your audience.

9. Long-term partnerships: While individual brand deals can be beneficial, building long-term partnerships with brands can provide more consistent income and mutually beneficial relationships. Establishing ongoing partnerships allows for deeper integration of the brand into your content and provides stability in terms of income and collaborations.

10. Legal and contractual considerations: It's important to review and understand the terms of any sponsorship agreements or contracts. If needed, consult with legal professionals to ensure the agreements protect your rights and outline clear expectations for both parties.

Remember, as a creator, your audience's trust should always be a priority. Choose sponsorships and brand deals that genuinely align with your channel's values and interests, and maintain transparency with your viewers. By nurturing relationships with brands and delivering valuable sponsored content, you can monetize your channel while preserving the integrity and authenticity that made your channel successful in the first place.

MERCHANDISE AND PRODUCT SALES

Merchandise and product sales can be a fantastic way to monetize your YouTube channel and engage with your dedicated fan base. By creating and selling branded merchandise or developing your own products, you can generate additional revenue while strengthening your brand. Here's a guide on leveraging merchandise and product sales for your YouTube channel:

1. Building a brand identity: Before diving into merchandise and product sales, it's crucial to establish a strong brand identity for your YouTube channel. Define your channel's unique personality, values, and target audience. Consistency in branding helps create a loyal and recognizable community that will be more likely to support your merchandise and products.

2. Identifying merchandise opportunities: Consider the types of merchandise that would resonate with your audience and align with your content. This can include branded apparel (e.g., t-shirts, hoodies), accessories (e.g., hats, stickers, phone

cases), or even digital products (e.g., e-books, presets, exclusive content). Analyze your viewers' preferences and engage with them through polls, comments, and social media to gather feedback and ideas.

3. Designing and producing merchandise: Collaborate with designers or create designs yourself that reflect your channel's brand and appeal to your audience. Ensure your merchandise is of high quality and visually appealing. Research reputable manufacturers or fulfillment services that can produce and ship your merchandise efficiently and at a reasonable cost.

4. Setting up an online store: Establish an online store where viewers can browse and purchase your merchandise. Several platforms provide user-friendly e-commerce solutions, such as Shopify, WooCommerce, or even integrated solutions like YouTube's merch shelf. Customize your store's layout, include clear product descriptions and high-quality visuals, and make the purchasing process straightforward and secure.

5. Promotion and marketing: Promote your merchandise through your YouTube channel, social media platforms, and other online channels. Create engaging content showcasing your merchandise, such as unboxing videos, look books, or testimonials from satisfied customers. Leverage your existing audience and engage with

them to create hype and anticipation around your merchandise launches.

6. Limited editions and exclusivity: Consider offering limited-edition merchandise or exclusive products to create a sense of scarcity and drive demand. This can incentivize viewers to make a purchase and can foster a sense of exclusivity within your community.

7. Partnering with influencers or collaborators: Collaborate with other YouTubers or influencers in your niche to cross-promote each other's merchandise. This can help expose your products to a wider audience and attract new customers who may be interested in your content and offerings.

8. Engaging with your community: Encourage your viewers to share photos or videos of themselves wearing or using your merchandise. Engage with them by reposting or featuring their content, holding giveaways, or offering discounts to loyal customers. This builds a sense of community and loyalty around your brand.

9. Customer service and fulfillment: Provide excellent customer service by promptly addressing inquiries, processing orders efficiently, and ensuring timely delivery. Maintain clear communication with customers regarding order status, shipping updates, and returns or exchanges. Positive customer experiences contribute to repeat purchases and word-of-mouth recommendations.

10. Continuous iteration and improvement: Regularly evaluate the performance of your merchandise and products. Gather feedback from customers, track sales metrics, and analyze customer preferences. Use this information to refine your product offerings, expand your merchandise line, and improve the overall customer experience.

Remember, while merchandise and product sales can be profitable, success often relies on building a loyal and engaged audience. Focus on creating valuable content, fostering a strong community, and delivering products that resonate with your viewers. By incorporating merchandise and product sales into your monetization strategy, you can diversify your revenue streams and strengthen your brand presence both on and off YouTube.

CROWDFUNDING AND DONATIONS

Crowdfunding and accepting donations from your audience can be an effective way to support your YouTube channel financially and connect more deeply with your viewers. By allowing your fans to contribute directly to your content creation efforts, you can access additional resources and build a stronger community. Here's a guide on leveraging crowdfunding and donations for your YouTube channel:

1. Understanding crowdfunding options: Crowdfunding platforms such as Kickstarter, Patreon, and GoFundMe offer different models to engage your audience and receive financial support. Research and select a platform that

aligns with your goals and allows you to provide value to your backers.

2. Identifying your funding needs: Determine the specific areas where financial support would benefit your channel. This could include improving video production quality, investing in new equipment or software, funding special projects, or supporting your overall content creation efforts. Clearly communicate your funding goals to your audience, highlighting how their contributions will directly impact the quality and quantity of your content.

3. Choosing the right crowdfunding platform: Select a crowdfunding platform that offers the features and benefits you desire. Consider factors such as platform fees, payment processing options, audience reach, and the ability to provide exclusive perks or rewards to your backers.

4. Creating compelling crowdfunding campaigns: Craft engaging and persuasive campaign pages that clearly articulate your channel's value proposition and the reasons why your viewers should support you. Explain how the funds will be utilized and what benefits backers will receive in return, such as early access to videos, exclusive content, personalized shout-outs, or merchandise discounts.

5. Promoting your crowdfunding campaign: Actively promote your crowdfunding campaign across your YouTube channel, social media platforms, and other online channels. Create dedicated

videos or promotional content that explains the campaign and encourages viewers to participate. Utilize eye-catching visuals, compelling storytelling, and clear calls to action to inspire your audience to contribute.

6. Providing exclusive rewards and perks: Incentivize your audience to contribute by offering exclusive rewards or perks to backers. These can include behind-the-scenes access, personalized messages, one-on-one consultations, private live streams, or exclusive merchandise. Tailor the rewards to suit different contribution levels, allowing viewers to choose the level of support that best suits their budget.

7. Engaging with your supporters: Show gratitude and appreciation to your backers by acknowledging their contributions publicly. Regularly update them on the progress of your projects or how their donations have directly impacted your channel. Engage with your supporters through personalized messages, responding to comments, or hosting special events exclusively for backers.

8. Accepting donations directly: In addition to crowdfunding platforms, you can also consider accepting direct donations from your audience through platforms like PayPal, Venmo, or Ko-fi. Provide clear instructions on how viewers can contribute and express your appreciation for any support received.

9. Transparency and accountability: Be transparent with your audience about how the funds are being used and provide regular updates on your channel's financial status. Building trust is crucial when accepting financial support, so ensure you maintain transparency and integrity throughout the process.

10. Compliance with regulations and tax obligations: Understand the legal and tax obligations associated with accepting donations or crowdfunding funds. Familiarize yourself with any relevant regulations in your region and consult with professionals if needed to ensure compliance with local laws.

Remember, crowdfunding and donations should be seen as an additional means of support, not a primary source of income. Focus on consistently delivering valuable content and building a strong community. By engaging your audience and providing opportunities for them to contribute, you can foster a sense of ownership and mutual support, allowing your channel to thrive and grow with the support of your dedicated fans.

UNDERSTANDING YOUTUBE'S POLICIES AND GUIDELINES

As a YouTube creator, it's crucial to familiarize yourself with YouTube's policies and guidelines to ensure that your channel remains compliant and doesn't face any unnecessary penalties or restrictions. By understanding and adhering to these guidelines, you can create a safe and positive environment for your viewers while avoiding potential issues. Here's an overview of some important YouTube policies and guidelines:

1. Community Guidelines: YouTube's Community Guidelines outline the rules and standards for content uploaded to the platform. These guidelines cover various aspects such as nudity or sexual content, harmful or dangerous content, violent or graphic content, hate speech, harassment, and spam. It's essential to review and understand these guidelines to ensure that your content meets the community standards.

2. Copyright and Fair Use: YouTube takes copyright infringement seriously. Familiarize yourself with YouTube's Copyright Policies, which prohibit the unauthorized use of copyrighted material. Understand the concept of fair use and how it applies to your content creation. If you include copyrighted material in your videos, make sure you have the necessary permissions or fall within the fair use guidelines.

3. Advertiser-friendly Content: YouTube has policies in place to ensure that content is suitable for advertisers. Advertiser-friendly content should be aligned with YouTube's guidelines and suitable for a wide range of advertisers. It's important to avoid controversial or sensitive topics, excessive profanity, violence, or any content that could be considered harmful or offensive to advertisers.

4. Monetization Policies: If you plan to monetize your YouTube channel, it's crucial to understand

YouTube's Monetization Policies. These policies cover requirements related to channel eligibility, adherence to YouTube's policies and guidelines, and compliance with the YouTube Partner Program terms and conditions.

5. Child Safety and COPPA Compliance: If your content is targeted towards children or has a significant audience of children, it's important to understand and comply with the Children's Online Privacy Protection Act (COPPA). YouTube has specific guidelines and requirements for content creators who produce content for children, including age-appropriate content and data collection restrictions.

6. Sponsored Content and Disclosures: If you engage in sponsored content or brand deals, it's essential to comply with YouTube's guidelines regarding disclosures. Clearly disclose any paid promotion or sponsorship in your videos or video descriptions to ensure transparency and comply with legal requirements.

7. Restricted Content: YouTube has specific restrictions on certain types of content, including explicit or adult content, violence, sensitive topics, and harmful or dangerous activities. Ensure that your content complies with these restrictions and is suitable for a wide range of audiences.

8. Terms of Service and Policies Updates: YouTube's Terms of Service and policies may be updated periodically, so it's important to stay

informed about any changes. Keep an eye on YouTube's official communications, notifications, or updates to ensure that your channel remains compliant with the latest policies.

9. Appeals and Dispute Resolution: If you believe that your content has been wrongly flagged or if you have any issues related to YouTube's policies or enforcement actions, familiarize yourself with the appeals and dispute resolution processes provided by YouTube. Understanding these processes can help you address any concerns or resolve issues effectively.

10. Ongoing Education and Community Support: YouTube offers resources, tutorials, and community forums where you can learn more about YouTube's policies and guidelines. Engaging with the YouTube creator community and staying informed about best practices can help you navigate the platform successfully.

Remember, YouTube's policies and guidelines are in place to maintain a safe and respectful environment for creators and viewers alike. By understanding and adhering to these policies, you can create content that complies with community standards, ensures advertiser-friendliness, and builds a positive reputation for your channel.

Chapter 8

GROWING YOUR CHANNEL AND INCREASING SUBSCRIBERS

Growing your YouTube channel requires a combination of creativity, consistency, and understanding your audience's preferences. It is a continuous process that involves both strategic planning and adapting to the ever-evolving YouTube landscape. As a content creator, one of your primary goals is to expand your reach and build a loyal audience that eagerly awaits your every upload. The following proven strategies and tactics will help you achieve steady growth and attract more subscribers to your channel.

ANALYZING YOUTUBE ANALYTICS

YouTube Analytics provides valuable insights into your channel's performance, audience engagement, and content effectiveness. By regularly analyzing these analytics, you can make data-driven decisions to optimize your content strategy, grow your audience, and increase viewer engagement. Here's a guide on how to analyze YouTube Analytics effectively:

1. Accessing YouTube Analytics: Sign in to your YouTube Studio dashboard and navigate to the Analytics tab. Here you'll find a wealth of data and metrics to analyze.

2. Overview and Channel Metrics: Start by reviewing the Overview section, which provides a snapshot of your channel's performance. Key metrics to look out for include views, watch time, subscriber count, and engagement metrics like likes, comments, and shares. Pay attention to any significant changes or trends in these metrics over time.

3. Audience Demographics: Explore the Audience section to understand the demographics of your viewers. Analyze data such as age, gender, and geographic location. This information helps you tailor your content to better serve your target audience and identify potential growth opportunities in specific regions or demographics.

4. Traffic Sources: The Traffic Sources section reveals how viewers discover and access your content. It shows which external platforms or websites are driving traffic to your channel, as well as the effectiveness of YouTube's suggested videos, browse features, or search results. This data helps you understand where your audience is coming from and optimize your content promotion strategies accordingly.

5. Watch Time and Audience Retention: Analyze the Watch Time and Audience Retention metrics to gauge how engaging your videos are to viewers. Identify videos with high watch time or those that experience significant drop-offs in viewer retention. Use this information to identify content patterns or topics that resonate well with

your audience and to improve the quality and length of your videos.

6. Content Performance: Dive into the Content section to analyze the performance of your individual videos. Look for trends in views, watch time, and engagement metrics across different videos. Identify your top-performing videos and explore what makes them successful. Use this insight to replicate successful content strategies and experiment with new ideas.

7. Playlists and End Screens: Evaluate the performance of playlists and end screens in the Interactions section. Determine which playlists generate the most views and engagement and optimize your playlists accordingly. Analyze the effectiveness of end screens in driving viewers to other videos or playlists and make adjustments to improve click-through rates.

8. Real-Time Data: Take advantage of the Real-Time section to monitor your channel's performance in real-time. This data is particularly useful when launching new videos or running time-sensitive promotions. Monitor the immediate impact of your content releases and make adjustments as necessary to maximize their visibility and engagement.

9. Experimentation and A/B Testing: Use YouTube Analytics to measure the impact of any changes or experiments you conduct. Test different video formats, titles, thumbnails, or content styles and compare the performance metrics to identify what

works best for your audience. This iterative approach helps you refine your content strategy and optimize for higher viewer engagement.

10. Goal Setting and Tracking: Set specific goals for your channel and regularly track your progress using YouTube Analytics. Whether it's increasing views, watch time, or subscriber count, having clear objectives helps you stay focused and measure your channel's growth over time. Adjust your strategies based on the insights gained from analytics to ensure you're on track to achieve your goals.

Remember, YouTube Analytics provides valuable data, but it's essential to interpret the metrics in the context of your channel's goals and audience. Regularly analyze and monitor your analytics to identify patterns, trends, and areas for improvement. By leveraging these insights, you can make informed decisions to optimize your content, grow your audience, and create a more engaging YouTube channel.

STRATEGIES FOR INCREASING SUBSCRIBERS

Gaining subscribers is a key milestone for any YouTube channel as it represents an engaged and loyal audience. Here are some effective strategies to increase your subscriber count and grow your YouTube channel:

1. Consistent and High-Quality Content: Consistently uploading high-quality videos is crucial for attracting and retaining subscribers. Create content that provides value to your target

audience, whether it's informative, entertaining, or both. Maintain a consistent upload schedule to keep your subscribers engaged and coming back for more.

2. Compelling Channel Trailer: Create a captivating channel trailer that highlights the unique value proposition of your channel. Use this opportunity to showcase your best content, introduce yourself, and explain why viewers should subscribe. Make it concise, engaging, and visually appealing to grab the attention of new visitors to your channel.

3. Engaging Thumbnails and Titles: Thumbnails and titles are the first things viewers see when browsing YouTube. Create eye-catching thumbnails that accurately represent your video's content and pique curiosity. Pair them with compelling titles that are both descriptive and enticing, encouraging viewers to click and watch.

4. Call-to-Action (CTA) End Screens: Utilize end screens in your videos to include a clear and compelling call-to-action for viewers to subscribe to your channel. Place the end screen strategically near the end of your videos to capture the attention of viewers who have enjoyed your content and are more likely to subscribe.

5. Compelling Channel Art and Branding: Create visually appealing and consistent channel art that reflects your channel's identity. A well-designed channel banner, logo, and overall branding create

a professional and memorable impression, making viewers more likely to subscribe and engage with your content.

6. Collaboration with Other YouTubers: Collaborating with other YouTubers in your niche can expose your channel to a new audience and help you gain subscribers. Look for opportunities to collaborate on videos, shout-outs, or joint projects that benefit both channels and provide mutual value to your audiences.

7. Cross-Promotion on Social Media: Leverage your social media presence to promote your YouTube channel and encourage your followers to subscribe. Share previews, behind-the-scenes content, or teasers of upcoming videos to generate excitement and drive traffic to your YouTube channel.

8. Engage with Your Audience: Responding to comments, interacting with your viewers, and building a sense of community fosters a loyal subscriber base. Encourage viewers to leave comments, ask questions, and share their thoughts. Engage with their comments and create a positive and interactive experience that makes them feel connected to your channel.

9. YouTube SEO: Optimize your videos for search engines by including relevant keywords in your titles, descriptions, and tags. Research popular keywords in your niche to improve your chances of appearing in search results, gaining visibility, and attracting new subscribers.

10. Promote Your Channel Outside of YouTube: Extend your reach by promoting your channel on other online platforms, such as your blog, website, or email newsletter. Cross-promote with other content creators, collaborate with influencers, or participate in relevant online communities to increase your channel's visibility and attract new subscribers.

11. Giveaways and Contests: Organize giveaways or contests that require viewers to subscribe to your channel for a chance to win. This incentivizes subscriptions and can create a buzz around your channel, attracting new viewers who are interested in participating.

12. Analyze and Learn: Regularly review your YouTube Analytics to understand which videos are performing well and attracting subscribers. Identify patterns, trends, and audience preferences to refine your content strategy and create more of the content that resonates with your viewers.

Remember, gaining subscribers takes time and effort. Focus on consistently delivering value, engaging with your audience, and optimizing your content strategy. By implementing these strategies and staying committed to creating high-quality content, you can increase your subscriber count and build a thriving YouTube channel.

YOUTUBE SEO FOR GROWTH

Search Engine Optimization (SEO) plays a crucial role in driving organic traffic to your YouTube channel and increasing your overall visibility on the platform. By optimizing your videos and channel for YouTube's search algorithm, you can improve your chances of appearing in search results and attracting new viewers. Here are some effective YouTube SEO strategies for growth:

1. Keyword Research: Conduct thorough keyword research to identify popular and relevant search terms in your niche. Use tools like Google Keyword Planner, YouTube's own search suggestions, and third-party SEO tools to discover keywords with high search volume and relatively low competition. Incorporate these keywords naturally into your video titles, descriptions, tags, and captions.

2. Optimized Video Titles: Craft compelling and keyword-rich titles for your videos. Include your primary keyword at the beginning of the title to increase its visibility. Make sure the title accurately reflects the content of your video and entices viewers to click and watch.

3. Detailed Video Descriptions: Write comprehensive and keyword-rich descriptions for your videos. Provide a summary of the video's content, include timestamps for different sections if applicable, and add relevant links to your website or other resources. Use your primary

keyword and related keywords naturally throughout the description.

4. Strategic Tags: Add relevant and specific tags to your videos to help YouTube understand the content and context of your video. Include a mix of broad and specific tags, including your primary keyword and related keywords. Use tags that are commonly searched by your target audience to increase the visibility of your videos in search results.

5. Closed Captions and Transcripts: Provide accurate and high-quality closed captions or transcripts for your videos. These not only enhance accessibility but also improve the overall searchability of your content. YouTube's automated captions may not always be accurate, so it's recommended to review and edit them manually.

6. Engaging Thumbnails: Create visually appealing and attention-grabbing thumbnails for your videos. A well-designed thumbnail can entice viewers to click on your video when it appears in search results. Use high-resolution images, vibrant colors, and text overlays to make your thumbnails stand out.

7. Playlists and Video Organization: Organize your videos into relevant playlists based on themes or topics. This helps viewers discover more of your content and encourages them to watch multiple videos on your channel, increasing watch time

and engagement. Use descriptive titles and keyword-rich descriptions for your playlists.

8. Encourage Engagement: YouTube values engagement signals such as likes, comments, and shares. Encourage your viewers to engage with your videos by asking questions, requesting feedback, or prompting them to share their thoughts in the comments. Engage with your audience by responding to comments and fostering a sense of community.

9. Promote External Backlinks: Promote your YouTube videos on other platforms, such as your website, blog, social media, or guest posts on other websites. Embed your videos in relevant blog posts or share them on social media platforms to drive traffic and generate external backlinks to your YouTube channel.

10. Monitor and Optimize: Regularly monitor your YouTube Analytics to gain insights into how your videos are performing. Analyze the watch time, audience retention, traffic sources, and viewer demographics to understand what's working well and identify areas for improvement. Use this data to optimize your future content and refine your SEO strategies.

Remember, YouTube SEO is an ongoing process. Continuously analyze and optimize your content based on viewer feedback, algorithm changes, and industry trends. By implementing effective SEO techniques and consistently delivering high-quality content, you can increase your visibility, attract new viewers, and drive growth for your YouTube channel.

LEVERAGING TRENDS AND EVERGREEN CONTENT

To grow your YouTube channel, it's important to strike a balance between leveraging current trends and creating evergreen content. By capitalizing on trends, you can tap into popular topics and attract new viewers. On the other hand, evergreen content provides long-term value and keeps your channel relevant even as trends come and go. Here's how you can leverage both strategies effectively:

1. Identifying Trends: Stay up-to-date with the latest trends, news, and events within your niche. Monitor industry-related websites, social media platforms, and YouTube itself to spot emerging topics or viral content. Keep an eye on trending hashtags, challenges, or viral videos that resonate with your target audience.

2. Timely Trend Videos: When you identify a relevant trend, create videos that address or capitalize on it. Provide your unique perspective, insights, or tutorials related to the trend. By releasing timely videos, you increase the likelihood of appearing in search results and gaining traction from viewers interested in the topic. Make sure to optimize your video titles, descriptions, and tags with relevant keywords.

3. Evergreen Content: Alongside trend-based videos, create evergreen content that remains relevant and valuable over time. Evergreen content addresses topics that have enduring interest and provides information, solutions, or entertainment that viewers can benefit from regardless of current trends. Examples include tutorials, educational content, product reviews, or in-depth discussions of fundamental concepts in your niche.

4. Keyword Research for Evergreen Topics: Conduct keyword research to identify evergreen topics that consistently attract search traffic. Look for keywords with steady search volume and relatively low competition. Create videos around these topics, optimizing your content with relevant keywords to increase visibility in search results.

5. Balancing Trend Videos and Evergreen Content: Strive for a balance between trend-based videos and evergreen content. Regularly schedule trend videos to take advantage of the immediate interest they generate, but also focus on creating evergreen content that continues to attract views and engagement over time.

6. Repurposing Trend Content: Some trends have a short lifespan, but their underlying concepts or themes can be repurposed into evergreen content. Identify the core value or lessons from past trend videos and create evergreen content around those concepts. This allows you to extend

the life of trend-based content and provide ongoing value to your audience.

7. Trend Spotting Tools: Utilize online tools and platforms that help you identify trends in your niche. Google Trends, YouTube Trends, and social media trend tracking tools can provide valuable insights into what's currently popular and what's gaining momentum. Stay proactive in monitoring these platforms to stay ahead of the curve.

8. Audience Engagement: Pay attention to your viewers' feedback and engagement metrics to understand their preferences. Take their suggestions, comments, and requests into consideration when planning your content strategy. Engaging with your audience and understanding their interests will help you create videos that resonate with them, whether they are trend-based or evergreen.

9. Timing and Consistency: To effectively leverage trends, release your videos promptly to maximize their impact. Timeliness is crucial for capitalizing on trends, as the interest and engagement around them can fade quickly. At the same time, maintain a consistent schedule for evergreen content, ensuring a steady stream of valuable videos for your audience.

10. Experimentation and Adaptation: Stay open to experimentation and adapt your content strategy based on the performance of trend videos and evergreen content. Analyze your YouTube

Analytics to understand what works best for your channel and adjust your approach accordingly.

By leveraging trends and creating evergreen content, you can attract both new viewers who are interested in the latest trends and long-term subscribers seeking valuable content. Finding the right balance between the two strategies will help you maintain relevance, attract a diverse audience, and foster sustainable growth for your YouTube channel.

Chapter 9

MANAGING YOUR YOUTUBE CHANNEL AND LONG-TERM SUCCESS

Building a successful channel involves effective management, organization, and the ability to adapt to the ever-changing digital landscape. There are key strategies and practices that will help you manage your YouTube channel effectively and lay the foundation for sustained growth and success. Managing a YouTube channel encompasses a wide range of responsibilities, from maintaining a consistent upload schedule to engaging with your audience and optimizing your content.

CONSISTENCY AND UPLOAD SCHEDULE

Consistency is a key factor in building a successful YouTube channel. Establishing a regular upload schedule helps you build trust with your audience, maintain their interest, and increase your chances of gaining subscribers. Here are some tips for maintaining consistency and establishing an effective upload schedule:

1. Set Realistic Goals: Determine how frequently you can realistically produce high-quality videos without compromising their quality. Consider factors such as your available time, resources, and the complexity of your content. It's better to

start with a modest upload schedule that you can consistently meet rather than overcommitting and struggling to deliver.

2. Plan Ahead: Create a content calendar or schedule to plan your video topics, production timelines, and release dates. This allows you to have a clear overview of your upcoming videos and ensures you have enough time to research, film, edit, and optimize each video before its scheduled release.

3. Consistent Day and Time: Choose specific days and times to release your videos and stick to them as much as possible. Consistency in your release schedule helps your audience anticipate and look forward to your new content. You can also use YouTube's scheduling feature to set the exact release time in advance.

4. Communicate with Your Audience: Let your audience know about your upload schedule. Mention it in your channel trailer, video descriptions, and on your social media platforms. This helps set expectations and encourages viewers to return for new content on specific days.

5. Quality over Quantity: While consistency is important, never compromise the quality of your videos to meet your upload schedule. Focus on delivering valuable, engaging, and well-produced content. It's better to release fewer high-quality videos than more mediocre ones. Your audience

will appreciate and respect your commitment to quality.

6. Batch Filming and Editing: Consider filming multiple videos in one session to save time and streamline your production process. This technique, known as batch filming, allows you to have a backlog of videos that can be edited and scheduled for release later. Just ensure that the topics and content remain relevant when they are published.

7. Utilize Buffer Periods: Allocate buffer periods in your schedule to account for unexpected circumstances or delays. Life happens, and unforeseen events can disrupt your production process. Having buffer periods allows you to maintain your upload schedule even if you encounter setbacks.

8. Monitor Audience Response: Pay attention to your audience's feedback and engagement metrics. Analyze which days and times generate the most views, likes, comments, and shares. This data can help you fine-tune your upload schedule to align with your audience's preferences and maximize engagement.

9. Adapt and Evolve: As your channel grows, you may need to adjust your upload schedule to meet the demands of your expanding audience. Analyze your YouTube Analytics to identify patterns in viewership and adjust your schedule accordingly. Don't be afraid to experiment with

different days and times to find what works best for your channel.

10. Be Transparent: If you need to make changes to your upload schedule, communicate it with your audience. Inform them about the reasons for the changes and provide an updated schedule. Transparency helps maintain trust and keeps your viewers informed.

Remember, consistency is key, but it's also important to prioritize the quality of your content. Find a balance between maintaining a regular upload schedule and delivering valuable videos that resonate with your audience. By being consistent, reliable, and providing content that meets your viewers' expectations, you can build a loyal subscriber base and foster the growth of your YouTube channel.

DEALING WITH COPYRIGHT ISSUES

Copyright issues can be a significant concern for YouTube creators. It's essential to understand and respect copyright laws to avoid potential penalties and account restrictions. Here are some tips to help you navigate copyright-related challenges on YouTube:

1. Educate Yourself: Familiarize yourself with copyright laws, especially those pertaining to your country or region. Understand the basics of copyright, fair use, and public domain. This knowledge will help you make informed decisions when it comes to using copyrighted material in your videos.

2. Create Original Content: Focus on creating original content that you own the rights to. This reduces the risk of copyright claims and allows you to have full control over your channel. Developing your unique style, format, and ideas will set you apart from others and minimize potential copyright issues.

3. Obtain Proper Licenses: If you want to use copyrighted material in your videos, obtain the necessary licenses or permissions from the copyright holders. This includes obtaining licenses for music, video clips, images, and other copyrighted material. There are platforms and services that provide royalty-free or licensed content specifically for YouTube creators.

4. Fair Use and Transformative Content: Understand the concept of fair use, which allows limited use of copyrighted material for purposes such as commentary, criticism, parody, or educational content. However, fair use is subjective and can vary depending on jurisdiction and the specific circumstances of each case. When using copyrighted material under fair use, provide proper attribution and context to support your transformative purpose.

5. YouTube's Content ID System: YouTube's Content ID system automatically detects copyrighted material in uploaded videos. If your video contains copyrighted content, you may receive a copyright claim or have certain restrictions placed on your video. Familiarize yourself with how the Content ID system works

and how to respond to copyright claims through YouTube's dispute process.

6. Use Royalty-Free and Creative Commons Material: Utilize royalty-free music, stock footage, images, and other creative commons-licensed content in your videos. These resources are specifically designed for use in content creation without infringing copyright. There are numerous websites and platforms where you can find such content, ensuring you have the necessary permissions to use them in your videos.

7. Editing and Transforming Copyrighted Content: When using copyrighted material, consider editing or transforming it in a way that adds significant value and makes it uniquely yours. This could involve adding commentary, conducting analysis, providing educational context, or creating transformative mashups. Adding your creative input can help strengthen your fair use argument and reduce the risk of copyright claims.

8. Monitoring and Responding to Claims: Regularly monitor your YouTube Studio for copyright claims or strikes. If you receive a claim, review the details and determine if it is valid. If you believe the claim is incorrect or falls under fair use, you can dispute it through YouTube's process. Be prepared to provide evidence and justification for your use of the copyrighted material.

9. Music Licensing Options: When using music in your videos, consider using licensed music from

platforms such as YouTube's Audio Library, which provides a wide range of free-to-use music tracks. Alternatively, you can explore music licensing platforms that offer affordable licenses for commercial use of popular music tracks.

10. Seek Legal Advice if Necessary: If you are uncertain about copyright laws or face complex copyright issues, it is advisable to seek legal advice from a qualified attorney who specializes in copyright law. They can provide personalized guidance based on your specific situation and help you navigate any legal challenges.

Remember, respecting copyright laws is crucial for maintaining a reputable YouTube channel. By focusing on creating original content, obtaining proper licenses, understanding fair use, and using royalty-free resources, you can minimize the risk of copyright issues and build a channel that thrives within legal boundaries.

HANDLING NEGATIVE FEEDBACK AND TROLLS

Negative feedback and dealing with trolls are common challenges that YouTube creators face. It's important to develop strategies to handle these situations effectively while maintaining your focus and positivity. Here are some tips for dealing with negative feedback and trolls:

1. Stay Calm and Composed: When encountering negative feedback or trolling comments, it's crucial to remain calm and composed. Take a moment to breathe and avoid responding impulsively or emotionally. Responding with

anger or defensiveness can escalate the situation and harm your reputation.

2. Assess the Feedback: Evaluate the feedback objectively and determine if it has any validity or constructive elements. Some negative comments may offer genuine criticism or suggestions for improvement. Use this feedback as an opportunity for growth and self-reflection. Disregard baseless or mean-spirited comments that provide no value.

3. Don't Take It Personally: Remember that negative feedback and trolling often have little to do with you personally. Internet trolls thrive on provoking reactions and stirring up conflict. Recognize that their comments are a reflection of their own issues, not your worth or talent as a creator. Developing a thick skin and not internalizing negative comments is essential.

4. Ignore or Delete Harmful Comments: In some cases, it's best to ignore negative or trolling comments entirely. Engaging with trolls can often perpetuate their behavior and give them the attention they seek. Alternatively, you can delete or hide harmful comments to maintain a positive and supportive environment on your channel. However, exercise caution and only remove comments that violate your community guidelines or contain hate speech.

5. Respond Professionally and Constructively: If you choose to respond to negative feedback, do so in a professional and constructive manner.

Address the issue with empathy, provide clarification or context if necessary, and thank the person for their input. Responding calmly and thoughtfully can diffuse tensions and demonstrate your professionalism to your audience.

6. Engage with Constructive Criticism: When you receive constructive criticism, embrace it as an opportunity for growth. Engage in a respectful dialogue with the person offering the feedback. Ask clarifying questions, express gratitude for their insights, and consider how you can incorporate their suggestions to improve your content. Constructive feedback can lead to positive changes in your channel.

7. Focus on Positive Feedback: Shift your focus to the positive feedback and supportive comments you receive. Recognize that the majority of your audience appreciates your content and values what you have to offer. Engaging with your positive and supportive viewers can help counterbalance the negativity and keep you motivated.

8. Seek Support from Your Community: Surround yourself with a supportive community of fellow creators, friends, and family members who can provide encouragement during challenging times. Lean on them for emotional support and advice when dealing with negative feedback. Having a strong support system can help you navigate difficult situations.

9. Moderating Comments: Utilize YouTube's comment moderation tools to filter and manage comments on your videos. You can enable comment approval or use filters to automatically hide certain words or phrases commonly associated with trolling or negativity. This allows you to maintain a more positive and respectful comment section.

10. Take Breaks and Self-Care: It's important to prioritize your mental well-being. If negative feedback starts to affect you emotionally, take breaks from reading comments or engaging with trolls. Engage in activities that help you relax, recharge, and refocus. Practice self-care to maintain a positive mindset and perspective.

Remember, negative feedback and trolls are inevitable parts of being a YouTube creator. Developing resilience, maintaining a positive mindset, and focusing on constructive feedback will help you grow as a creator and create a positive environment for your audience. Stay true to yourself, and don't let negativity discourage you from pursuing your passion on YouTube.

SCALING YOUR CHANNEL AND TEAM

As your YouTube channel grows, you may find it necessary to scale your operations and expand your team. Scaling effectively can help you manage the increased workload, maintain the quality of your content, and further grow your channel. Here are some strategies for scaling your YouTube channel and building a team:

1. Assess Your Needs: Evaluate your current workload, content production requirements, and areas where you need support. Identify tasks that can be delegated or outsourced to free up your time for higher-value activities. This could include video editing, graphic design, social media management, or community engagement.

2. Define Roles and Responsibilities: Clearly define the roles and responsibilities of each team member to ensure everyone understands their contributions. Identify the key skills and expertise needed for each role and hire or assign team members accordingly. This will help streamline your operations and ensure efficient collaboration.

3. Hire or Collaborate with Specialists: Consider bringing in specialists or collaborators who excel in specific areas relevant to your channel's growth. For example, you may need a dedicated video editor, a graphic designer, or a social media manager. Look for individuals who are passionate about your niche and share your vision for the channel's growth.

4. Establish Communication and Workflow Systems: Implement effective communication and workflow systems to streamline collaboration and ensure everyone is on the same page. Use project management tools, communication platforms, and shared calendars to keep everyone organized and informed. Regular check-ins and meetings can help align goals and address any challenges.

5. Delegate and Empower Your Team: Delegate tasks and responsibilities to your team members based on their skills and strengths. Empower them to make decisions and take ownership of their respective areas. Trusting your team and giving them autonomy will not only relieve your workload but also foster a sense of ownership and motivation.

6. Provide Training and Support: Invest in training and development opportunities for your team members to enhance their skills and stay updated on industry trends. This can include workshops, online courses, or industry conferences. Providing ongoing support and mentorship can also help your team members grow both personally and professionally.

7. Maintain Quality Control: As you scale, it's crucial to maintain the quality standards that your audience expects. Develop guidelines and style guides to ensure consistency across your content. Regularly review and provide feedback on your team's work to ensure it aligns with your channel's brand and vision.

8. Foster Collaboration and Creativity: Encourage collaboration and creativity within your team. Foster an environment where team members feel comfortable sharing ideas, experimenting with new approaches, and contributing to the channel's growth. Collaboration can lead to fresh perspectives and innovative content ideas.

9. Adapt and Iterate: Be flexible and willing to adapt your team structure and processes as your channel evolves. Regularly assess your team's performance and identify areas for improvement. Seek feedback from your team members and your audience to identify new opportunities and refine your strategies.

10. Nurture a Positive Team Culture: Foster a positive and supportive team culture where everyone feels valued and motivated. Celebrate successes, recognize team members' contributions, and provide opportunities for growth and advancement. A positive team culture will not only enhance productivity but also contribute to the long-term success of your channel.

Scaling your YouTube channel and building a team requires careful planning and effective management. By delegating tasks, hiring specialists, establishing clear communication, and fostering a positive team culture, you can effectively scale your operations while maintaining the quality and growth of your channel. Remember, building a strong team is an investment that can propel your YouTube channel to new heights.

Chapter 10

THE FUTURE OF YOUTUBE AND KEEPING UP WITH TRENDS

The digital landscape is constantly evolving, and YouTube is no exception. It is crucial to stay informed about the latest advancements, features, and shifts in user behavior to make informed decisions for your channel. In this final chapter, we will explore the future of YouTube and the importance of staying ahead of trends. As a content creator, it is essential to adapt and evolve with the ever-changing digital landscape to maintain your relevance and sustain long-term success.

EMERGING YOUTUBE TRENDS

Staying abreast of emerging YouTube trends is crucial for keeping your channel relevant and engaging for your audience. By embracing new trends, you can captivate viewers, attract new subscribers, and stay ahead of the competition. Here are some of the emerging YouTube trends to watch out for:

1. Short-form Video Content: With the rise of platforms like TikTok and Instagram Reels, short-form video content has become increasingly popular. Consider creating bite-sized videos that are concise, visually captivating, and shareable. Experiment with formats like quick tips, tutorials, behind-the-scenes glimpses, or entertaining

snippets to cater to viewers' shorter attention spans.

2. Live Streaming and Interaction: Live streaming allows you to connect with your audience in real-time, fostering a sense of community and interactivity. Consider hosting live Q&A sessions, behind-the-scenes streams, or interactive challenges to engage with your viewers. Live chats and audience participation can make viewers feel more connected and involved.

3. Niche and Specialized Content: As YouTube continues to expand, catering to niche audiences has become increasingly important. Consider specializing in a specific topic or subgenre within your niche to attract a dedicated fan base. Delve deeper into your niche by creating content that addresses specific interests, concerns, or hobbies, providing unique value to your viewers.

4. Authenticity and Storytelling: Viewers appreciate authenticity and relatability. Share personal stories, experiences, and challenges to connect with your audience on a deeper level. Authenticity fosters trust and loyalty, and viewers are more likely to engage with creators they feel a genuine connection to.

5. Educational and How-to Content: YouTube is a popular platform for learning, and educational content continues to thrive. Create tutorials, how-to guides, or informative videos that offer valuable insights and teach your viewers something new. Focus on providing actionable tips, step-by-step

instructions, or in-depth knowledge on a specific subject.

6. Sustainability and Eco-conscious Content: As environmental consciousness grows, so does the interest in sustainability-related content. Consider incorporating eco-friendly practices and sharing tips on sustainable living, zero waste, ethical consumerism, or eco-conscious lifestyles. Addressing these topics can attract an audience passionate about making a positive impact on the environment.

7. Vlogging and Personal Journeys: Vlogs and personal journey videos remain popular as viewers enjoy getting glimpses into the lives of their favorite creators. Share your daily experiences, travel adventures, or personal challenges. Vlogs provide a more intimate and authentic connection with your audience.

8. ASMR and Relaxation Content: Autonomous Sensory Meridian Response (ASMR) videos have gained significant popularity. These videos aim to trigger a soothing and relaxing sensation through soft sounds, gentle whispers, or visual stimuli. Experimenting with ASMR or relaxation content can attract viewers seeking a calming and immersive experience.

9. Interactive and Gamified Content: Engage your audience with interactive and gamified content that encourages participation. This could include quizzes, challenges, polls, or interactive storytelling. Give your viewers the opportunity to

actively engage with your videos, making them feel like a part of the experience.

10. Virtual Reality (VR) and 360-degree Videos: VR and 360-degree videos provide immersive and unique viewing experiences. Explore creating content that takes advantage of these technologies to offer viewers a sense of being physically present in different environments or situations.

Remember, trends evolve rapidly, so it's essential to stay open to experimentation and adapt to the changing landscape. Monitor industry news, keep an eye on popular channels, and listen to your audience's feedback to identify emerging trends that align with your channel's niche and goals. By embracing emerging YouTube trends, you can stay relevant, attract new viewers, and continue to grow your channel.

STAYING RELEVANT IN AN EVER-CHANGING PLATFORM

YouTube is a dynamic platform that constantly evolves, making it essential for creators to stay relevant to maintain their audience engagement and channel growth. Here are some strategies to help you stay relevant in an ever-changing YouTube landscape:

1. Keep Up with Trends: Stay informed about current trends, both within your niche and on the platform as a whole. Regularly explore popular videos, trending topics, and viral content to understand what resonates with viewers.

Embrace relevant trends by creating content that aligns with them, putting your unique spin on them to cater to your audience.

2. Conduct Audience Research: Continuously study your audience to understand their interests, preferences, and needs. Use YouTube analytics to gather data on viewership demographics, watch time, and engagement metrics. Pay attention to comments, messages, and feedback from your audience to gain insights into what they want to see. Tailor your content to meet their expectations.

3. Experiment with New Formats: Don't be afraid to try new content formats and styles to keep your channel fresh and engaging. Test different video lengths, storytelling techniques, editing styles, or visual effects. Experimenting helps you discover what works best for your audience and keeps them excited to see what you'll do next.

4. Collaborate with Other Creators: Collaborations with other YouTubers can expose you to new audiences and bring fresh perspectives to your content. Seek out collaborations with creators who share a similar target audience or have complementary content. Collaborative videos can introduce your channel to new viewers and offer exciting content variety.

5. Engage with Your Community: Foster a strong connection with your audience by actively engaging with them. Respond to comments, messages, and social media interactions

promptly and authentically. Host Q&A sessions, polls, or contests to encourage audience participation and make them feel involved in your channel. Building a loyal community helps maintain relevance and sustains channel growth.

6. Diversify Your Content: Explore different content types to cater to various viewer preferences. Incorporate a mix of educational, entertaining, inspirational, or personal content. Offer a range of formats such as tutorials, challenges, vlogs, or interviews. Diversifying your content helps you appeal to a broader audience and keeps your channel dynamic.

7. Stay Active on Social Media: Extend your online presence beyond YouTube by actively engaging on social media platforms. Promote your videos, share behind-the-scenes glimpses, and interact with your audience on platforms like Instagram, Twitter, or Facebook. Building a strong social media presence increases your visibility and helps you connect with viewers outside of YouTube.

8. Attend Industry Events and Conferences: Stay connected with the YouTube community by attending industry events, conferences, or meetups. Networking with other creators, industry professionals, and YouTube representatives can provide valuable insights and opportunities. Stay updated on platform changes, best practices, and emerging trends through industry events and workshops.

9. Seek Feedback and Adapt: Regularly seek feedback from your audience, fellow creators, or trusted mentors. Be open to constructive criticism and use it to improve your content and channel strategy. Stay flexible and willing to adapt to audience preferences, platform updates, and industry shifts. Being responsive to changes ensures your relevance and keeps your channel thriving.

10. Invest in Continuous Learning: The YouTube landscape is ever-changing, so invest in continuous learning to stay ahead. Stay updated on algorithm changes, SEO strategies, content creation techniques, and industry best practices. Attend webinars, enroll in online courses, or join creator communities to expand your knowledge and skills.

By implementing these strategies, you can adapt to the ever-changing YouTube platform and maintain relevance in the eyes of your audience. Embrace new trends, engage with your community, diversify your content, and stay informed to continue growing your channel and staying relevant in the competitive YouTube ecosystem.

EXPERIMENTING AND EVOLVING YOUR CHANNEL

In the fast-paced world of YouTube, it's crucial to continually experiment and evolve your channel to keep it fresh, engaging, and aligned with the ever-changing interests of your audience. Here are some strategies to help you experiment and evolve your channel effectively:

1. Set Clear Goals: Define your goals and vision for your channel. Determine what you want to achieve, whether it's increasing subscribers, improving engagement, or expanding into new content areas. Clear goals will guide your experimentation and help you measure the success of your channel's evolution.

2. Analyze Audience Feedback: Pay attention to your audience's feedback, including comments, messages, and social media interactions. Listen to their suggestions, requests, and constructive criticism. Use this feedback to identify areas for improvement and potential avenues for experimentation.

3. Try New Content Formats: Explore new content formats to provide variety and cater to different viewer preferences. Consider trying formats like vlogs, tutorials, challenges, reaction videos, or storytelling. Experimenting with different formats can help you discover what resonates best with your audience and keeps them engaged.

4. Collaborate with Other Creators: Collaborations with other YouTubers can introduce fresh perspectives and expand your reach. Look for opportunities to collaborate with creators in your niche or related niches. Collaborative videos can bring new viewers to your channel and provide exciting content for your existing audience.

5. Introduce New Segments or Series: Introduce new segments or series within your channel to add structure and consistency. This could be a weekly Q&A session, a monthly favorites video, or a special series related to your niche. These recurring segments create anticipation among your viewers and encourage them to regularly tune in.

6. Incorporate Viewer Interaction: Actively involve your audience in your channel's evolution by seeking their opinions and ideas. Conduct polls, surveys, or contests to gather feedback and encourage participation. By incorporating viewer interaction, you make your audience feel valued and invested in your channel's growth.

7. Stay Up-to-Date with Trends: Keep an eye on emerging trends within your niche and on YouTube as a whole. Stay informed about popular topics, content styles, and editing techniques. Experimenting with trending content can help you stay relevant and attract new viewers who are interested in current trends.

8. Embrace New Technologies and Features: Be open to embracing new technologies and features on YouTube. For example, explore incorporating live streaming, 360-degree videos, or virtual reality content if it aligns with your channel's niche and audience interests. Adopting new technologies can set your channel apart and provide unique experiences for your viewers.

9. Monitor Analytics and Metrics: Regularly review your channel's analytics and metrics to gain insights into viewer behavior, video performance, and audience demographics. Pay attention to metrics like watch time, retention rate, and audience engagement. This data can guide your experimentation and help you make informed decisions about your channel's evolution.

10. Stay True to Your Brand: While it's essential to experiment and evolve, always stay true to your channel's brand and core values. Maintain consistency in your messaging, content quality, and visual style. Your audience expects a certain level of authenticity and familiarity, so ensure that your experiments align with your overall brand identity.

Remember, experimentation and evolution are ongoing processes. Continually assess the results of your experiments, learn from them, and refine your content strategy accordingly. Stay open to feedback, adapt to changing trends, and never be afraid to take calculated risks. By experimenting and evolving your channel, you can keep your audience engaged, attract new viewers, and ensure long-term success on YouTube.

CONCLUSION

Throughout this book, we have covered a wide range of topics and provided you with valuable insights, strategies, and tips to help you embark on your YouTube journey. Starting a YouTube channel is an exciting endeavor, but it also requires dedication, creativity, and perseverance. We have explored the rise and popularity of YouTube, the various types of YouTube channels, and why starting a YouTube channel can be a lucrative business opportunity.

You have learned how to research and analyze your target audience, define your unique selling proposition, and set up your YouTube channel with engaging channel art, branding, and optimized settings. We have also delved into planning your content, creating compelling videos, and enhancing them through editing.

Engaging with your audience, collaborating with other YouTubers, and leveraging social media and SEO strategies have been highlighted as important elements for growing your channel. We have also discussed monetization options such as the YouTube Partner Program, sponsorships, merchandise sales, and crowdfunding.

Understanding YouTube's policies, analyzing YouTube analytics, and strategies for increasing subscribers and maximizing growth have been covered in-depth. We have emphasized the importance of staying relevant, handling copyright issues, dealing with negative feedback, and scaling your channel with a team.

Finally, we explored emerging YouTube trends, staying consistent with upload schedules, and navigating challenges like copyright issues and negative feedback. We concluded by highlighting the importance of experimenting and evolving your channel to keep it fresh and engaging.

Remember, success on YouTube doesn't happen overnight. It requires persistence, adaptability, and continuous learning. Use the knowledge and strategies you've gained from this guide to carve your path and make a lasting impact on YouTube.

As you embark on your YouTube journey, always stay true to yourself, be authentic, and provide value to your audience. Embrace your creativity, follow your passion, and don't be afraid to take risks. With dedication, hard work, and a willingness to learn and adapt, you can build a successful and profitable YouTube channel.

Wishing you the best of luck on your YouTube channel! Remember to enjoy the process and have fun creating content that resonates with your viewers. Here's to your success as a YouTube creator!

www.ingramcontent.com/pod-product-compliance
Lightning Source LLC
La Vergne TN
LVHW051246050326
832903LV00028B/2597